America Armed

ESSAYS ON UNITED STATES MILITARY POLICY

RAND McNALLY PUBLIC AFFAIRS SERIES

America

Essays on United

BY

ROBERT E. OSGOOD
WALTER MILLIS
HERMAN KAHN
JOSEPH CROPSEY
DAVID R. INGLIS
MULFORD Q. SIBLEY

Armed

States Military Policy

EDITED BY

ROBERT A. GOLDWIN

RAND McNALLY & COMPANY • CHICAGO

RAND McNALLY PUBLIC AFFAIRS SERIES

America Armed: Essays on United States Military Policy
A Nation of States: Essays on the American Federal System
Why Foreign Aid? Essays on United States Economic Aid Policy

PREFACE

●

Thermonuclear war has been widely spoken of as "unthinkable." The meaning of that assertion has never been perfectly clear (for the same public leaders who made the pronouncement continued policies that prepared us to fight such a war, if necessary). And yet the statement does convey a meaning, or perhaps several meanings. It means, at least, that it is beyond human powers to imagine the extent of the suffering and destruction nuclear war would cause. It suggests, further, that nuclear war will not happen unless we begin to think that there might, some time, be reasons to make it happen. Prolonged thinking about nuclear war might accustom us to its horrors; familiarity might lessen our dread, making us less unwilling to use nuclear weapons when provoked. The conclusion is that we must not think about the possibilities, lest that very act of thinking itself cause the dread catastrophe.

The present essays are six attempts to think about the "unthinkable." The authors reject the ostrich's posture; they offer instead models of courageous, reasoned inquiry, with no shrinking from the harshest realities. Their efforts are to understand, to clarify, and, where possible, to illuminate the way for those who must make the decisions that bind us all. The authors all find that the low level of our present understanding is incommensurate with the awesome urgency and magnitude of our perils.

The basic questions are clear. Is there an escape from the moral dilemma: peace at the price of surrender or defense of all that is decent in this world at the risk of global obliteration? Can we use our military power to further our cause without destroying what we seek to defend? Or has military power become obsolete; that is, has it become useless in the work of solving the world's major problems? Is there any way that we can accomplish disarmament without exposing ourselves, unarmed at the critical moment, to a deceitful, still-armed enemy? And, finally, if some means is not soon found to limit or eliminate arms, where will it all end?

The authors agree that these are the questions; they disagree in their answers. Readers have no alternative but to choose among them, according to their own lights. It is not an exaggeration to say that our national survival and, indeed, the fate of all mankind depend in very great measure on how well we choose.

R. A. G.

January 1963

CONTENTS

●

The authors themselves are alone responsible for the opinions expressed and the policies recommended in their respective papers. The Public Affairs Conference Center is a nonpartisan, educational institution and as such takes no position on questions of public policy.

THE EDITOR AND THE AUTHORS

•

ROBERT A. GOLDWIN

is Lecturer in Political Science and Director, Public Affairs
Conference Center, University of Chicago. His books include
Readings in World Politics, 5th ed., 1959; *Readings in Amer-
ican Foreign Policy,* 5th ed., 1959; and *Readings in Russian
Foreign Policy,* 3rd ed., 1959.

ROBERT E. OSGOOD

is Professor of American Foreign Policy, School of Advanced
International Studies, and Research Associate, Washington
Center of Foreign Policy Research, Johns Hopkins University. His fields of specialization are American foreign and
military policy and international relations. He is the author
of *Ideals and Self-Interest in America's Foreign Relations,*
1953; and *Limited War:The Challenge to American Strategy,*
1957.

WALTER MILLIS

a military historian, is a Member of the Staff of the Center
for the Study of Democratic Institutions. A former editorial
and staff writer for the New York *Herald Tribune,* he has
written *The Martial Spirit,* 1931; *Road to War,* 1935; *Why
Europe Fights,* 1940; *The Last Phase,* 1946; *This is Pearl!,*
1947; and *Arms and Men,* 1956. He also edited *The Forres-
tal Diaries,* 1951.

The Authors

HERMAN KAHN

Director and Member of the Executive Board, Hudson Institute, was formerly on the Research Staff of RAND Corporation as a strategic analyst. A consultant to the Department of Defense and other governmental agencies, he is the author of *On Thermonuclear War*, 1960; and *Thinking About the Unthinkable*, 1962.

JOSEPH CROPSEY

is Assistant Professor of Political Science, University of Chicago. His fields of specialization are economics and political philosophy. He is the author of *Polity and Economy*, 1957.

DAVID R. INGLIS

is a Senior Physicist at Argonne National Laboratory. From 1957 to 1958 he was a physicist with the European Organization for Nuclear Research (CERN), Geneva, Switzerland. A former Chairman of the Federation of American Scientists, he is the author of *Testing and Taming of Nuclear Weapons*, 1960.

MULFORD Q. SIBLEY

is Professor of Political Science, University of Minnesota. His special field of interest is political theory. He is co-author of *Conscription of Conscience*, 1952; co-editor of *Personality, Work, Community*, 3rd ed., 1961; and author of *Unilateral Initiatives and Disarmament*, 1962.

ROBERT E. OSGOOD

•

THE USES OF MILITARY POWER
IN THE COLD WAR

The following analysis is confined to the next decade or two, partly because this is as far as I can anticipate relevant military and political developments and partly because, whatever problems the decades beyond may hold, I believe that our opportunity to deal with them successfully, or at all, will depend critically upon the way we deal with those that we can see developing now.

The unstable, unregulated nature of the contemporary international system and the revolutionary and militant nature of Communist society make the capacity to wage war an indispensable instrument of national survival and of a just international order. Military power cannot, in the foreseeable future, be abolished, any more than conflict among sovereign states, of which it is a primary symptom and tool, can be abolished. Yet the immense destructive power of modern weapons makes war itself a highly volatile and potentially self-defeating instrument of policy. Therefore, the overriding task of modern statecraft is to restrain military power and control it for legitimate political ends. If we shun this exacting task on the assumption that military power has become irrelevant to the preservation of legitimate national and international values (either because it is impossible to control or because it will control itself) we shall certainly lose these values through peaceful erosion and probably through piecemeal or wholesale violence.

To protect national interests and promote a just international order, America's military power must serve three functions: It must deter aggression; if deterrence fails, it must defeat aggression by means sufficiently limited to serve political ends;

and it must support national policy by means short of war. To fulfill these three functions, America's military power must operate within an international military balance so stable, and with forces so susceptible to prudent discipline, that the incidence and magnitude of warfare will be sufficiently limited to avoid disrupting the rudimentary equilibrium among states that enables them to pursue their competing aims and interests and to satisfy their basic security requirements without destroying the state system itself. We must recognize, however, that the achievement of this equilibrium will not stabilize an inherently unstable international society. It will only channel the present profound competition into a struggle for power largely by nonmilitary means, and in that struggle, military power will continue to play a decisive role through its political and psychological impact.

Before we examine the concrete requirements of military power, a brief survey of the contemporary international system and of Communist doctrine and practice will show that the capacity to wage war has become more, not less important as a means of supporting national policy and ordering international relations.

On the one hand, the conflicts among nations are more profound and virulent than in any other period of the modern state system. This is so not only because of the massive organized power of two revolutionary Communist states, but also because of the explosion of indigenous revolutions in what used to be called the backward areas, revolutions which are at once nationalist, social, economic, and racialist in character. On the other hand, the nonmilitary means of regulating and moderating international conflict have never been less adequate for the task. The regulating mechanisms that preserved a reasonably stable balance-of-power system in the eighteenth and nineteenth centuries—countervailing alliances and alignments, secret diplomacy, colonialism, economic subsidies, dynastic changes, and the like— have withered away. They have withered away because the conditions that made them work—principally, a fairly equal distribution of power among a number of states, limited war potential, a rudimentary ethical consensus among rulers and ruling classes, and ready access to territorial compensations—have been destroyed by the polarization of power, popular nationalism, ideological conflict, the spread of Western industrial technology, and the immense destructive potential of modern weapons.

As a means of preserving stability with justice in the present international anarchy, the United Nations is a weak substitute for the regulating mechanisms of the past. It is no substitute at all for the national management of military power, except for the occasional use of an *ad hoc* international police force to establish order or preserve a truce with the consent of the major powers.

The importance of military power as an instrument of national policy is enhanced by the fact that the Communist states have a vested interest in stimulating international instability as a transitional stage to their own ideal of a stable "socialist world system" of states and by the fact that they regard military power, both in doctrine and practice, as an indispensable instrument for achieving it. Their doctrinal analysis of reality abounds with avowals of the crucial importance of armed coercion in advancing the power of the Party, as long as non-Communist states exist. The extension of Communist control and influence has depended critically on the organized use of military power by overt and tacit means. By doctrine and experience the Communist powers approach military power with calculated circumspection, always utilizing it as an integral part of a total configuration of power, and always subordinating it to overriding political purposes. They have been quick to capitalize upon the new conditions of military power, which are congenial to the political exploitation of arms short of war and by indirect and limited means.

In recognition of the catastrophic nature of unlimited war, Communist leaders have repudiated the "fatal inevitability" of the elimination of the capitalist powers by warfare. The Soviet Union has conceded that a general war would be a disaster to the Communist cause, even though Communist society would survive and capitalist society would perish. The Communist powers have said, however, that the utility of other forms of warfare will depend on whether the non-Communist societies can be eliminated or absorbed by peaceful means. They have agreed that "national-liberation wars" are inevitable as long as capitalism exists, and that the Communist powers must support them "wholeheartedly and without reservations." They envisage the growth

3

of Soviet nuclear power as having produced a decisive shift in the over-all military balance, which must lead the capitalist camp to withdraw its protection from vulnerable forward positions like Berlin and Laos. And they maintain immense modern military establishments capable of warfare of every type and scope (except for the temporary absence of a Chinese nuclear capability). In employing this vast and diversified panoply of military power, the Chinese are, in this phase of the cold war, more adventurous in utilizing limited and paramilitary warfare, but the Russians display consummate skill and boldness in exploiting their military potential as an instrument of political warfare.

We must appreciate, therefore, that the novel destructiveness of modern weapons has not diminished the role of military power. It has only altered and complicated that role, while actually enlarging it. The nonmilitary mechanisms for maintaining the state system through an equilibrium of power have withered away. Yet in the absence of an effective *preponderance* of power in the hands of one state or a supranational organization, only an *equilibrium* of power can preserve order and justice in the face of contemporary international conflicts. Today such equilibrium must be based largely on a military balance. Yet the extreme destructive potential of warfare has made the traditional instrument and test of military balance—an armed contest—a possibly catastrophic, if sometimes unavoidable, recourse. This situation has increased the importance of the nonviolent uses of military power, as a deterrent and as an instrument of political warfare and diplomacy. (Arms have always been most useful when they were not used.) It has enhanced the attractiveness, for the aggressor, of limited, paramilitary, and subversive methods of violence. For aggressor and defender alike it has put an unprecedented premium on the deliberate limitation of all forms of overt armed conflict.

The United States and her allies, approaching military power with principles and experience radically different from the Communists', have been slow to recognize and respond to the new conditions of military power. Yet they have proclaimed—even if they have oversimplified—the importance of deterrence, and they have acknowledged—even if they have not fully acted upon—the importance of limiting warfare. In practice their actions and inactions in the cold war have been a tacit recognition of the pervasive but subtle role of military power. If they do not explicitly comprehend the full nature of this role, the area of freedom will either deteriorate or vanish in thermonuclear explosions. But if it does, this will not be because of any inevitable tendencies springing from the nature of military technology, the international system, or even Communist strategy but, rather, because of a failure of democratic intelligence and will.

If armed force is to serve as an effective instrument of national policy and of a just international order, the great task of modern statecraft in the next decade or two is to expand an area of mutual restraints upon the use of military power within an over-all field of antagonistic interests and aims—to achieve essential forms of "co-operation" within unavoidable configurations of conflict. Restraint joined with antagonism and cooperation joined with conflict are common modes of international relations and, indeed, of all spheres of social and political relations. When modes of conflict-and-restraint persist long enough, they may acquire a social, political, and even moral sanction that gives them the status of customs and rules of conduct and, in their most stable form, the status of laws and administrative procedures.

Yet the revolutionary impact of the radically new instruments of armed struggle which have appeared so suddenly in recent decades makes it implausible that the modes of military conflict in this century can evolve into anything but the most rudimentary and tentative rules of conduct. Furthermore, the depth and intensity of the central political conflict in the cold war, *added* to the volatile, catastrophic potential of modern warfare, cast doubt upon the feasibility of *any* modes of conflict-and-restraint controlling the instruments of violence that this "century of total war" will produce.

On the other hand, there are at least two conditions that make such control more feasible than in the preceding part of this century. First, the Communists are highly circumspect about the overt use of military power and especially cautious about using it in a direct and massive way. Secondly, the major contenders in the cold war recognize and have manifestly acted upon novel incentives to avoid the uncontrolled use of military power. In other words, there are dangers of catastrophic warfare, implicit in the nature of modern military technology, which the major powers recognize a mutual interest in mitigating, despite their basic political hostility. Therefore, it is not surprising that, so far, the great powers have employed warfare and the threat of warfare with a restraint that is entirely unprecedented in the history of such profound political and ideological conflict.

However, the depth and intensity of this political and ideological conflict, and the distrust which it breeds, severely limit the utility of formal agreements as instruments of military restraint and co-operation. The usefulness of the formal control of arms is further limited by a rapidly changing military technology, which continually alters the material basis of a mutually acceptable military balance. There may be some feasible as well as desirable kinds of formal arms control which embody specific procedures for verification and specific modes of co-operation that cannot be provided by informal and tacit understandings; but in the next decade or two, the area of military restraint and co-operation must be enlarged and stabilized chiefly by reciprocal unilateral arms controls and by informal and tacit understandings. For these measures have a flexibility, simplicity, discreetness, and ambiguity more suitable to the rudimentary, fragile, and tentative modes of mutual restraint in the cold war than formal agreements publicly committing the signatories to detailed terms of co-operation.

Many formal arms agreements that have been proposed seem analogous to attempts to regulate social and economic relationships with laws when there is no stable social or economic basis for their support. Accordingly, they would probably only exacerbate distrust, misunderstanding, and tension. Only those agreements that are integral parts of diplomatic accommodations, that mitigate the political sources of tension, seem likely to be constructive. The most useful formal arms agreements, therefore, would facilitate a political settlement by adjusting the military balance to sustain a new configuration of power; for example, a regional military withdrawal and arms limitation accompanying a reunification of Germany. But by the same token, the same arms agreement without an adjustment of political relationships could be a fertile source of tension and war.

The most significant nonformal measures to stabilize the military balance will be those that can be taken unilaterally, either unconditionally or contingent upon reciprocity: for example, refraining from needlessly provocative dispositions of weapons, renouncing policies that would lead to countermeasures disadvantageous to both parties, establishing clear lines of military command and political control, announcing and implementing strategies congenial to the limitation of force, and developing weapons systems that permit gradations and discrimination in the use of force, that provide time for deliberation, and that minimize the risk of being used by accident and misapprehension. Most of such measures would be beneficial whether or not they were reciprocated. Some would require more or less explicit bargaining and negotiation. All would depend on effective communication between governments, by the language of actions as well as of words—if only by improvised restraints such as those that kept the Korean War limited.

The control of military power by these means would be merely an extension of the mutual restraints that have already operated in the cold war. It would not *eliminate* the terrible risks and dangers of military power, or transform the struggles for power into a polite game. We must recognize, however, that to the extent these measures should succeed in mitigating the instability of the military balance and the volatility of warfare, the capacity to wage war would lose some of the terror of *uncontrollable* violence, which is undoubtedly a deterrent to armed conflict. Yet, surely, this is a price well worth paying for the rational control of military power.

The primary and indispensable instrument of military equilibrium in contemporary international relations is deterrence, that is, the discouraging of a hostile act by manipulating the fear of military counteraction. The phenomenon of military deterrence is as old as the state system itself, and even older; but never before has the security of nations depended so much upon it, and never before has deterrence depended upon such exacting and sophisticated calculations and such unremitting technological effort. The inherent difficulty of determining the kinds of military counteractions that will convince potential adversaries that the risks and penalties of various kinds of aggression would outweigh anticipated benefits, combined with the diversity of possible weapons systems from which to choose, their high cost, and limitations upon the allocation of financial and scientific resources to military purposes (especially in democratic countries), impose a severe burden of strategic planning upon governments. Yet there is now an emerging consensus in the United States on the principal requirements of deterrence; and the prospects in the next decade or two of stable deterrence, at least in the realm of deterring nuclear warfare, are not unpromising.

Briefly, the essential requirement for deterring a direct assault on the United States is a sufficiently invulnerable retaliatory (or second-strike) force to inflict unacceptable damage on the aggressor. To avoid the absolute necessity of having to strike only at civilian targets (a necessity that would probably foreclose the possibility of negotiating an end of the war without capitulation or complete catastrophe), such a second-strike force should also include some "counterforce" capability; that is, a capability of striking at military targets, especially missiles and bombers and command centers. But a counterforce capability intended to "win the war" through protracted nuclear exchanges makes no sense.

If a civil-defense program has any value, it is simply to minimize civil damage, as a concomitant of a second-strike capability, not to enhance the credibility of our striking first.

In the next decade the development of reliable, concealed, and mobile strategic weapons promises to give both the USA and the USSR a sufficiently invulnerable retaliatory force to restrain either from initiating strategic nuclear attacks upon the other. It also promises to create a situation approaching mutual nuclear sufficiency, which will moderate the quantitative nuclear weapons race, although the qualitative competition in research and development will and should continue as a protection against one-sided technological innovations that might undermine the adequacy of second-strike forces.

The Uses of Military Power in the Cold War

Under these conditions one can envisage the USA and the USSR reaching a tacit understanding that neither power would try to build a sufficient counterforce capability to deliver a first strike that could confine retaliatory damage to acceptable levels, as long as the other side refrained from trying to build such a force. The understanding would be self-enforcing in the sense that either party could unilaterally detect a violation—that is, an attempt by the other party to build an adequate counterforce capability for a first strike—and either could redress it by expanding his retaliatory force at much less effort than the violator would have to undertake to achieve an advantage. Despite its ambiguity and lack of precision—indeed, because of these qualities—such an understanding would be more reliable and, technically and politically, more feasible and useful than a formal agreement designed to stabilize the deterrent balance and control the arms race by the limitation and inspection of strategic weapons. For a treaty would not only be difficult to negotiate, verify, and enforce; it would also be subject to rapid technological obsolescence and all the suspicion and annoyance accompanying an effort to freeze a dynamic military balance in formal and detailed restrictions.

The stabilization of mutual deterrence of strategic first strikes would, however, jeopardize America's deterrence of non-nuclear aggressions upon her allies in so far as such deterrence depended on the threat of initiating nuclear warfare. Indeed, the strategy of "massive retaliation" against conventional Soviet aggression has long since ceased to have much credibility, although it may still be sufficiently credible to constitute a vital marginal deterrent against direct armed attacks on America's European allies.

To offset the dwindling credibility of a nuclear first strike in response to aggression against other powers, America's proper course is not to try to restore this credibility by emphasizing her strategic counterforce superiority or by undertaking a huge civil-defense program, for she would thereby unstabilize the strategic balance and accelerate the arms race without creating a more useful first-strike force. Rather, the United States and her allies should enlarge their capacity for effective resistance by limited

9

nonnuclear warfare, reserving both tactical and strategic nuclear weapons as deterrents against the adversary's using them first.

Deterrence, however, would not be foolproof. Even the achievement of adequate second-strike and limited-resistance capabilities is probably not sufficient to assure the mutual deterrence of direct military action. It would be extravagant to suppose that governments will always be so clairvoyant and circumspect as to restrain each other and themselves from resorting to war. Yet at least they must and can minimize the danger of *nuclear* war resulting from an *accident* or from *misapprehension* that an adversary intended to resort to nuclear war.

One source of this danger lies in the existence of offensive strategic weapons so accurate, fast, and powerful as to induce a country that fears a nuclear attack to deliver a pre-emptive blow, in order to save its retaliatory capability, before accurately appraising the evidence of an attack. Another source is the danger of technical and personal malfunctions that would cause missiles or planes to be launched contrary to the intentions of the government. But these sources can be readily controlled by creating sufficiently invulnerable striking forces to permit adequate reaction time and to minimize dependence on early warning, by establishing effective central control and command of nuclear weapons, and by instituting mechanical and organizational safeguards against unauthorized use.

The central source of war by misapprehension and accident lies in the decisions of governments, not in weapons as such. The source of war by misapprehension lies, particularly, in strategies and acts that might provoke a pre-emptive blow. These include not only such acts as the launching of seemingly threatening bomber flights and the harassing of enemy retaliatory capabilities, but also strategies that avowedly depend on initiating the use of nuclear weapons. The way to guard against these dangers is to refrain from provocative acts, clarify nonoffensive intentions, reduce strategic dependence on nuclear responses to conventional aggression, and renounce (or at least de-emphasize) first-strike strategies. If nuclear war results from accidents, despite mechanical and organizational safeguards against technical and personal malfunctions, governments can at least respond to accidents in ways that will prevent their leading automatically to all-out war. They can do so by adopting strategies and capabilities that provide sufficient opportunity for political control and deliberation in the retaliatory use of nuclear weapons. Obviously, it would be advantageous to secure Soviet co-operation in providing mutual assurance against nuclear attacks that might arise from misapprehension or accident. But most of the required measures would be advantageous even if they were undertaken unilaterally. In a more stable, cohesive international society, mutual assurance against surprise attack might be served better by formal agreements which specified, elaborated, and verified the modes of military co-operation, so that the parties to the agreement would have reliable tests of mutual restraint—especially during crises, when informal co-operation and communication might break down. But in the present international anarchy and the present atmosphere of well-founded international suspicion it is doubtful that mutual assurance of peaceful intentions can be more readily achieved by precise and explicit formal tests than by ambiguous and tacit informal tests. Rather, the formal tests, in proportion to their complexity, are likely only to increase the opportunities for, and therefore the suspicions of, the dissembling of intentions and the manipulation of the modes of co-operation for hostile purposes. If only because of their high rate of technological obsolescence, elaborate international inspection and surveillance schemes would be peculiarly susceptible to subversion or simple misunderstanding, so that, in proportion to the co-operation they required, they might actually incite the fear and suspicion they were intended to allay. It would be extremely difficult, furthermore, to devise a system of inspection that would give an adversary assurance against surprise attack without also giving him information on the numbers and locations of missiles and bombers, information that would facilitate *his* launching a surprise attack.

In any case, as long as the West feels compelled to reserve—if only as a deterrent—the ultimate possibility of initiating the use of nuclear weapons rather than acquiescing in a nonnuclear defeat, it should not commit itself to formal arrangements designed to provide assurance against a first strike. A nation that wishes to avoid provoking a pre-emptive first strike but is not prepared completely to renounce its own resort to nuclear war against nonnuclear aggression must strive to achieve some balance between assuring the adversary that it does *not* intend to strike first in some circumstances and convincing him that it *might* strike first in others. A formal commitment to procedures designed for the first purpose would be distinctly uncongenial to such a balance.

If the United States and her allies took the proper unilateral measures, a tolerably stable state of mutual deterrence of at least nuclear first strikes could be achieved between the NATO powers and the Soviet Union. However, the diffusion of nuclear capabilities to Communist China and to powers not aligned with either bloc would certainly be a far more serious source of instability.

This paper cannot analyze the precise nature of these sources of instability or discuss the measures to counter them, but it is clear that, if the process of nuclear diffusion is to be halted with any assurance, it must be halted by formal arms agreements—including a nuclear test ban, a nuclear production cut-off and prohibition, and a ban on nuclear transfers—which would entail rather elaborate measures of restriction, verification, and enforcement. Yet these agreements seem quite unlikely to be accepted, and equally unlikely to work satisfactorily if they were accepted, despite a presumed common interest between the USA and USSR in their objective. Perhaps the surest way to prevent nuclear diffusion is to bring about universal nuclear disarmament, but, for reasons which I cannot expound here, a safe and stabilizing agreement of this sort is out of the question.

But whether or not formal agreements to halt nuclear diffusion should prove feasible, stable bipolar nuclear deterrence can reduce the pace and hazards of diffusion. For to the extent that the major nuclear powers have, in effect, confined nuclear weapons to second-strike deterrents designed only to prevent the other side from using nuclear weapons, and to the extent that they have reduced the risk of nuclear war by accident and misapprehension, the incentives for potential nuclear powers who are not motivated by offensive political aims to acquire nuclear capabilities or to use them actively and rashly will be minimized. To prevent those powers who do have offensive political aims from pursuing them with nuclear weapons, only some kind of policing agreement between the two major nuclear powers (who would have a keen interest in preventing nuclear war)—say, as a minimum, a mutual understanding that neither would oppose the other's restraining threat or action against the offending third party—would offer any hope of preserving a modicum of stability.

It should be added that the task of impeding nuclear diffusion should start at home, with NATO. The diffusion of the independent production and ownership of nuclear weapons among the allies would not only encourage similar diffusion outside the alliance; it would also undermine allied cohesion without enhancing allied security. Yet probably the only hope of preventing such diffusion of *production* without straining allied cohesion by trying to retain an Anglo-American nuclear monopoly, lies in sharing the *control* of nuclear weapons under NATO auspices— at least to the extent of joint planning and consultation. Above all, it lies in reducing the dependence of all the allies on a nuclear first-strike strategy.

It would be imprudent to assume that any system of military deterrence could provide absolute security against war. It can provide very significant assurance against the grosser forms of warfare, and it can minimize the danger of lesser forms expanding out of control. But there will remain virulent sources of internal revolution and subversion and of hostilities among non-bloc powers, which will produce wars to which military deterrence is inapplicable and in which major bloc powers may wilfully or reluctantly, directly or indirectly, become involved. Moreover, given the fallibility of human calculation and the incidence of irrationality, the possibility of a breakdown of mutual deterrence—even premeditated strategic nuclear warfare—cannot be excluded from our military planning.

This does not mean, however, that we must assume that all armed conflict must inevitably lead to a completely unlimited spasm of violence. Rather, we must assume that it is imperative to prevent *every* armed conflict from reaching catastrophic dimensions. Considering the acute awareness of all the present nuclear powers of the utter uselessness of unlimited warfare, it would be disastrously fatalistic to assume that technological possibilities compel them to use force without any restraint or discrimination. Rather, we must assume that even in the event of strategic nuclear exchanges they would have a great incentive, and might develop some means, to stop short of mutual annihilation.

It follows that we must adopt strategies and acquire capabilities that will hold open rather than foreclose the opportunity of imposing meaningful limits even on strategic nuclear warfare. These must include moderate civil-defense and counterforce capabilities and an announced and planned strategy of graduated or proportional nuclear blows—that is, controlled rather than unlimited retaliation—together with an effective system of central command and control of nuclear weapons. Otherwise, we shall virtually guarantee that every nuclear attack—no matter what its magnitude, targets, source, circumstances, or consequences—will become an unmitigated catastrophe. The chief purpose of such preparations, however, would not be to make either tactical or strategic nuclear warfare an active instrument of policy—any nuclear warfare is too likely to get out of control for that—but simply to be prepared in case others initiate nuclear blows, to terminate the war without surrendering or committing suicide.

Yet it is more immediately and urgently important to prepare for local nonnuclear warfare; for, whereas the stability of mutual nuclear deterrence decreases the likelihood of nuclear attacks, it increases the likelihood of limited nonnuclear aggressions and "national-liberation wars," which could, in turn, expand (or "escalate") into nuclear war. We cannot exclude the possibility of limited war even in Europe. Surely, in the division of Berlin and Germany there are political sources of such a conflict. Outside Europe the Communist powers have publicly proclaimed their new opportunities for exploiting revolution to gain control of peripheral points formerly protected by American nuclear power, which, they boast, is now neutralized by Soviet nuclear power.

The Uses of Military Power in the Cold War

The Chinese have asserted territorial claims which they are determined to satisfy by military means, if necessary. They and their satellites have been practicing a well-developed strategy of indirect aggression, which rests on the organized use of armed coercion integrally related to political penetration—after the pattern of Communist operations on the Chinese mainland and in the Philippines, Burma, Malaya, Indochina, Laos, and South Vietnam. Their acquisition of an independent nuclear capability is bound to encourage an even more adventurous use of this strategy. At the same time, the political instability of the whole colonial and formerly colonial area in Asia, the Middle East, and Africa makes it ripe for indigenous armed conflicts, which, regardless of whether they are incited or sustained by China or Russia, will impinge on the vital interests of the great powers and threaten to involve them in war.

So far, the basic deterrent to a more active and open use of limited armed aggression by the Communists in these areas has been less the protective umbrella of American nuclear power than the vulnerability of the local governments and societies to nonmilitary incursions. This deterrent, however, does not recommend itself as a policy. The policy that does recommend itself—and with considerable urgency—is a well-conceived counterstrategy of political influence, designed to bolster rather than undermine political stability, supported by a diversified capacity for limited and "sublimited" military resistance. And if the Communists threaten to overrun the receding periphery of the free world without the overt employment of armed force, the West should not flinch from countering such aggression with its own military and paramilitary operations, where the political conditions are appropriate.

I subscribe to the current consensus that, on grounds of military effectiveness as well as susceptibility to limitation, our advantage lies in depending as much as possible on a nonnuclear limited-war capability and as little as possible on the resort to "tactical" nuclear warfare. However, it would be irresponsible to renounce all recourse to nuclear weapons before we have a larger capability for nonnuclear resistance. On the other hand, when we have acquired a large enough conventional capability to raise the threshold of our effective limited resistance to a level

15

and scope of violence to which the use of nuclear weapons would add only a moderate and credible gradation, we will not *need* to renounce recourse to nuclear weapons in order to deter and defeat aggression.

My conclusion is that it would be foolishly unrealistic and contrary to all the evidence to suppose that armed conflict has somehow been expunged from the revolutionary political upheavals in the world. But it would be fatally imprudent to be unprepared to protect the vital interests of the free world by meeting limited and indirect forms of armed conflict and aggression with comparably limited and indirect resistance. That has already proved to be essential and possible. It will be no less so in the foreseeable future.

Surely, it is more plausible to suppose that great powers, who know they have nothing to gain and everything to lose from an all-out war, will be circumspect in the use of force than that they will inevitably use force to the utmost. If we follow those who contend that war is "unthinkable" or "obsolete" because it must inevitably be too extreme to serve any rational or moral purpose, we shall not thereby avoid warfare. We shall only invite the outbreak of armed conflict and aggression while foreclosing the possibility of meeting it with any middle course between capitulation and catastrophe.

If we can achieve a stable balance of mutual nuclear deterrence and succeed in limiting, if not deterring, nonnuclear conflict, this will neither terminate the cold war nor resolve the political upheavals that would exist even in the absence of the cold war. But the basic competition of interests and aims between the two blocs will then be directed into nonmilitary channels, and the impact of revolutionary forces at work outside the blocs will be somewhat pacified. However, the mitigation or even the complete elimination of armed conflict would not eliminate the influence of military power in international relations. It would only emphasize the role of arms as a tacit instrument of policy, a role which has already assumed a prominence far greater than is recognized by our traditional view of military power. For the inhibitions toward using modern weapons, combined with the absence of nonmilitary mechanisms for regulating power politics, have made the political and psychological exploitation of military power a dominant method of conducting international relations.

There is an analogy here to Von Clausewitz's description of the limited wars of political maneuver in the eighteenth century:

> Thus war became essentially a regular game in which time and chance shuffled the cards; but in its significance it was only diplomacy somewhat intensified, a more forceful way of negotiating, in which battles and sieges were the diplomatic notes. To obtain some moderate advantage in order to make use of it in negotiations for peace was the aim of the most ambitious.

Now it is the *prospect* of war rather than the "battles" and "sieges" themselves that constitutes "diplomacy somewhat intensified."

Of course, there is nothing new about the offensive and defensive exploitation of military power by means short of war; but this exploitation acquires a new psychological dimension when it depends, ultimately, upon the prospect of nuclear obliteration—when it depends so heavily upon manipulating the threat of unacceptable civilian damage rather than upon simply confronting the enemy with a capacity to defeat his forces on the battlefield or at sea. For then it involves the nerves and the will and morale of whole nations in a direct and perhaps decisive way.

George F. Kennan has observed that "armaments are important not just for what could be done with them in time of war, but for the psychological shadows they cast in time of peace." One should add that the psychological shadows armaments cast in time of peace are shaped largely by what men think could and would be done with them in time of war. Today much of international politics is basically concerned with interpreting and casting these shadows.

The Communists, being attuned by doctrine and experience to the political and psychological overtones of military power, have readily capitalized upon the new opportunities to exploit their prospective victims' anticipation of war. With great resourcefulness they use the fears of war projected by nuclear weapons and their own immense military strength, together with their adversaries' longing for peace and normality, to sustain a well-tried tactic of alternating tensions and peaceful détentes. This tactic is designed to test the resolution and cohesion of their adversaries, to gain, if possible, an easy political or diplomatic triumph, to isolate a vulnerable power and humiliate its protector, and, above all, to divide the Western alliance.

The phrase by which we commonly describe Russia's offensive use of armed force by tacit means is "nuclear blackmail," but even this relatively simple and direct use of the threat of war is more subtle and diffuse than the phrase implies. The most conspicuous form of nuclear blackmail depends on Russia's conveying the implication that she will launch punitive nuclear blows unless other powers cease "provocative" and "aggressive" acts. She used such threats in the Suez War of 1956, the Syrian crisis of 1957, the Quemoy and Matsu crisis of 1958, after the U-2 incident in 1960, and during the consolidation of the Cuban revolution in 1960. However, they were all carefully timed, qualified, and rendered ambiguous; and it is doubtful that they had much effect on their ostensible objects, although in the eyes of others they undoubtedly helped present the USSR as a powerful champion of the "zone of peace" against the reactionary designs of the "capitalist-imperialists."

A more effective, if less direct form of blackmail depends not on the threat of *Soviet* first strikes, which is not likely to be plausible, but on the threat that nuclear war might result from a *Western* response to limited and ambiguous Communist incursions. For, in this circumstance, the onus of nuclear war can be more readily placed upon the prospective victims instead of the perpetrators of aggression, and the victims are more likely to be divided in their response. Therefore, the preferred tactic of the Communist powers is to place their adversaries in a position in which they must anticipate either a peaceful compromise on Communist terms or else a choice between ineffective resistance or a disastrous nuclear war. Nothing is so antithetical to the cohesion of an alliance or to the maintenance of a firm, specific, and concerted diplomatic position as the necessity of having to anticipate such a choice, even if the armed conflict that would compel it should never occur. Nothing is so conducive to brinkmanship, to a diplomacy of bluff and counterbluff, with all the attendant hazards of recklessness and miscalculation, as having to depend on a military capability that would be futile or self-defeating if it had to be used.

Khrushchev has made it alarmingly clear that he believes that, with the addition of a devasting Soviet nuclear capability to huge and diversified conventional forces, a fundamental shift in the world military balance has taken place, so that in his opinion American-protected outposts along the Sino-Soviet periphery, such as Berlin and Laos, are no longer tenable. Since the United States and her allies, he declares, will not now dare intervene against the "forces of peace and democracy" at the risk of incurring the penalties of nuclear war, they must withdraw their protection or suffer the consequences. To the extent that the Western powers must extend their protection by nuclear means or not at all, Khrushchev may be right. But whether or not the West really lacks the will and capability to protect the vital outposts of freedom, the crucial danger is that the Soviet and Chinese leaders may *believe* that it does and act accordingly.

The NATO nations have learned that the test of effective military power is not only to win a battle but to deter a battle, but they have been slow to grasp the more subtle and diverse political and psychological uses of military power. From the Western standpoint, nuclear deterrence is the prerequisite for protecting the status quo from violent change; but from the Soviet standpoint, it is the prerequisite for extending the Communist sphere of control and influence (Khrushchev's definition of the status quo) at a tolerable risk by nonviolent means. To the Western powers, international tensions are bad because they disturb normal relations and threaten to erupt in war; therefore, these powers strive, above all, to eliminate specific sources of tension in a step-by-step approach to peace. But to the Communist leaders, the raising or lowering of tensions and the threat of war are merely tools of policy, because they regard the underlying source of tensions and war—that is, the existence of the capitalist camp —as ineradicable until the capitalist states, step-by-step, are buried. In liberal democratic eyes, war is the opposite of peace, as conflict is distinguished from the absence of conflict. But in

Robert E. Osgood

Communist eyes, war and peace are distinguished merely as differing methods of waging an inexorable class conflict, in which summit conferences, disarmament proposals, ban-the-bomb campaigns, subversion, economic and military assistance, space demonstrations, "peace offensives," and war or the threat of war are all tactical elements of an integrated strategy of conflict.

To suppose that, in all this tactical maneuvering, the balance of military power and the vision of war play no part, is to ignore the daily realities of the cold war and the Communists' own diagnosis of them. The Communists prefer to attain their ends without armed conflict and to keep armed conflict limited or paramilitary if war should be expedient, but, manifestly, they also understand the multifarious uses of military potential in securing peaceful acquiescence. There is no reason to think that the spread of technical education in the Soviet Union, the desire for consumer goods, the bureaucratization of the government, the economic squeeze of armaments, or the fear of general war will dissuade the Russians from pressing their success with this method of aggrandizement, even if they are less adventurous than their Chinese allies in the overt use of force.

The military part of the remedy for this politico-military threat is as obvious as it is difficult for democratic nations to adopt. It is not only to proclaim and support the stability of nuclear deterrence as a major goal of military policy, but also to build a sufficiently large and diversified nonnuclear capability to avoid having to choose between ineffective resistance and nuclear war and to support vital political positions without bluff. Such a capability is feasible as well as essential for the NATO powers to achieve. And from the standpoint of American interests and values the NATO area is still the single most important area in the cold war. However, outside Europe such a capability must depend more on indigenous forces, and in these areas there may not always be a suitable political and material basis for effective local resistance. But that does not mean that a capacity for organized military resistance is unimportant in such cases; it means that this kind of capacity, to be effective, must rest on what Mao Tse-tung calls a solid base of "political mobilization."

The Uses of Military Power in the Cold War

Of course, a suitable military posture is not by itself a sufficient counter to a politico-military threat. Although there are new dangers of war inherent in the nature of military technology itself, military threats and conflicts still spring from human decisions, and from political incapacity and turmoil. Therefore, the West must have a strategy of political as well as military stability in order to foster a relatively peaceful and orderly transition of national and international society in this revolutionary age. To counter the Communist strategy of exploiting political instability, manufactured tensions, and the propaganda of peace and détente, we must have a program for guiding nationalist ambitions and economic and social aspirations into a constructive set of new relationships. And we must formulate genuinely negotiable and just diplomatic positions that would mitigate the real political sources of tension, such as the division of Berlin and Germany. But these tasks are not a substitute for the wise and vigilant management of military power. They are integrally dependent on a military posture that can deter the extremities of violence without provoking it, and that can defend free peoples without obliterating them.

Admittedly, the approach to the control of military power that is proposed here is principally a holding operation, designed to go as far as seems feasible by *military* means toward restraining and pacifying the international environment in the next decade or two. We must recognize that the ultimate agents of civilized order and justice are not to be found in military measures, whether they are designed to increase, abolish, or merely stabilize military power. Yet if the major Western powers can survive and prosper in the foreseeable period of intense cold war and political and social revolution with the help of the measures suggested here, they may also have developed, as a by-product of this effort, not only new military controls and restraints, but also some new nonmilitary mechanisms for regulating whatever political and institutional modes of international relations the rest of the twentieth century may unfold.

WALTER MILLIS

●

THE USELESSNESS OF
MILITARY POWER

The present international order and its power relationships
are founded upon a military concept of power which has been
an anachronism at least since 1916 and totally unworkable
since 1945. To say, with Robert Osgood, that "the unstable, unregulated nature of the contemporary international system and
the revolutionary and militant nature of Communist society
make the capacity to wage war an indispensable instrument of
national survival and of a just international order," is, I submit, to misread the nature of modern war, the requirements of
national survival, and even the nature of Communist aims and
strategy.

Since the end of the eighteenth century, the international
order, like the domestic, has of course undergone profound
transformations. We have been compelled to accept radical alterations in almost every institutional aspect of our lives—political, social, familial, economic—save one. Our military institutions, with the concepts which support them and the emotions
which surround them, are still essentially those of the Western
or Atlantic world of the late eighteenth century. On the eve of
the French Revolutionary and Napoleonic eras the war system
had developed into a brutal yet reasonably practicable and
tolerable mode for the conduct of international power relationships. The nations, or at least their governing elites, contended
over dynastic, territorial, or commercial issues;[1] when such issues
became acute, a war occurred, but it seldom put much strain

[1] Many would add "ideological issues" as well. I omit them because the
ideology has always seemed to me much more an expression of the politics than
the politics an expression of ideology.

22

on the societies involved. It was war "limited" as to aims and means; it was waged by professional officers and relatively small numbers of riffraff and "pressed" men; the effects upon the societies which they represented were minimal. Large tracts of territory, particularly colonial territory, might change hands; power positions rose and fell, but the Western international order in 1793 did not differ significantly from that of a century before.

By 1815 the political, technological, and even moral foundations of this international order had been seriously eroded. The peace made at Vienna recognized many great social and political changes; but it accepted the eighteenth-century war system as the "natural" and immutable mode in the relations of nation-states. The Western powers engaged in about as many wars in the hundred years after 1815 as they had in the hundred years before. The ideological, emotional, and institutional settings surrounding these conflicts were the same as before. Yet history and technology were imposing their modifications. In the eighteenth century the great European military powers challenged each other to open combat with slight hesitation; and the wars, however limited in means, were great-power conflicts, whose outcome settled great-power issues. After the grim experiences with Napoleon there was an increasing tendency to use, not war itself, but the *threat* of war as a means of maintaining the national defense or advancing the national interest. The powers tended to hypothecate their military power and influence, as it were, in order to secure results without being required actually to pay down on the barrel-head. Clausewitz's celebrated comparison of actual war to a commercial "settlement day" (a comparison which would hardly have occurred to an eighteenth-century writer on warfare) suggests the trend. The many wars of the nineteenth century can generally be classified as colonial wars, civil wars (e.g., the Carlist wars in Spain), or wars of national unification (in Germany, Italy, the United States, and Latin America). Even when such "peripheral" wars erupted, as in the Crimea or the Franco-Prussian War, into conflicts between major military states, they remained "limited" in character (and consequences). The international war system, which had operated with relative freedom and success in the eighteenth century, was by the nineteenth beginning to generate certain "contradictions" within itself which were already at least calling it in question. Since Napoleon I, there had been many wars but no great war in Europe; partly, no doubt, because under the developing social, political, and technological changes taking place, war was becoming increasingly inappropriate as a means of conducting the relations of the modern nation-states.

It was better to confide the national security and interest to the "balance" of military power rather than to its exertion. Diplomacy devoted itself to maneuvering for strategic position as a hedge against the future rather than to threatening military force to secure immediate ends. The nineteenth-century colonial wars are of interest as reflections of this European strategic power struggle rather than responses to a desire for the dubious rewards of imperial expansion. The French invaded Algeria in 1830 less because of a need for anything in Algeria than because their governing elite needed to fortify their military power and prestige in Europe by invading somebody, and they could no longer invade the Germanies as Napoleon had done. A very similar motivation was to produce Mussolini's military descent upon Ethiopia a century later. The partition of Africa after 1880 was primarily impelled, not by a lust for African resources, but by questions of prestige in Europe, of European power positions and by strategic calculations against the possibility of a war in Europe. So far as the European power balance was concerned, the African scramble really represented a military form of what is now called "indirect aggression."

But the more nicely the balances were adjusted, the more unstable they were obviously becoming, and the more costly and dangerous the instabilities which they were themselves generating. At the turn of the century the Polish banker Ivan Bloch, noting the effect of the magazine rifle and the new automatic weapons at such slaughters as that of Omdurman, suggested that technology was rendering war impossible. His ideas are credited with inspiring the first call to disarmament, issued by the Imperial Russian Government in 1898. This summons accurately prophesied that at the rate things were going the proliferating and competitive armaments would produce the very catastrophe they were designed on all sides to prevent. Nothing, of course, came of the resultant Hague Conference of 1899—the attempt to maintain a peaceful balance of military power turned out to be self-defeating—but the notion that the whole system of competitive armament and military threat was obsolescent had been implanted in many minds, notably including those of Alfred Nobel and Andrew Carnegie. The Russo-Japanese War of 1904–5 bore out many of Bloch's ideas about the military and political effects of the new weaponry; the ghastly trench stalemate in Europe, 1915–17, seemed to bear out the underlying implication that war had become "impossible" for any human purpose. After 1918 there were millions to believe that the war system was not only obsolescent but obsolete.

In fact, it was. What was still in its essentials an eighteenth-century concept of international power relations had totally broken down under the novel conditions of the twentieth. An international order which had seemed to work at least tolerably well through the century after Waterloo had in fact been working remorselessly to its own destruction. Every compromise adjustment which saved it for the time being only made ultimate disaster more certain. The competitive armaments and military diplomacies of the early twentieth century were all basically defensive and conservative in intent, yet all ended in a gigantic and revolutionary catastrophe which no one wanted, no one planned, and from which few if any really benefited. As a mode in which to conduct the external relations of the great modern states, the war system was both useless and intolerable.

The creation of the League of Nations and the disarmament efforts of the interwar years were recognitions of this fact. They were attempts to revolutionize the international order. They failed—in part perhaps because their authors did not themselves realize how profound was the revolution they were proposing, as the peoples who applauded them certainly did not. The old order remained, modified only slightly by the new concepts of collective security and the new, hopefully more stable, military alliance systems set up to buttress it. One can only speculate as to what might have happened had the victors in 1918 been able to act upon the truth which was already evident; if they had sought to abolish war rather than simply to demolish the German war machine, and if they had disarmed themselves as they were disarming the Germans. The results for human history could hardly have been worse than those which actually ensued. As it was, the victors fell back upon a conventional concept of military power which was already outmoded, and the inutility of which was soon and tragically to be demonstrated. Relying upon their predominant military power and alliance systems, France and Britain (with or without the United States) would keep Germany permanently harmless. No doubt the objective was laudable. The difficulty with it was not its unwisdom but its impracticability. Even massively superior military power was not, after 1918, an effective instrument for imposing or maintaining that kind of international stability.

The situation had barely been restored, at Locarno, to a tolerably stable state when Adolf Hitler arose in Germany to challenge it. His object was to destroy the *"diktat"* of Versailles and establish Germany as the predominant "power" in Europe. What this goal really meant to Hitler—and even what it means today to those who ascribe it to him—is not readily understandable. There are those who contend that "power," in the abstract, is a meaningless concept, that it acquires content only in relation to the purposes for which it is used. Hitler never clearly explained his ultimate purposes and perhaps never fully rationalized them to himself. As with many other revolutionaries, the purposes seemed to serve the acquisition of power, rather than that power was acquired in order to further purposes. But in any event, if the assumed equivalence of national military power—formed armies and fleets and going industrial base—with national power is valid, Hitler's attempt to gain "dominance" could not have succeeded.

He took control of a virtually disarmed and bitterly divided nation, with its war industry dismantled, and through it challenged the power of the world's two strongest military states. But their military strength proved useless to them. As A. J. P. Taylor shrewdly observes, while Germany was disarmed she offered no practicable *military* target to the French (the Ruhr occupation demonstrated that), while by the time the creation of the Reichswehr had provided one, Franco-British military superiority was gone. Ten years after Locarno, with the reoccupation of the Rhineland in 1936 (an operation which Hitler's military advisers told him was militarily impossible), the *"diktat"* was annulled; the Versailles system had been destroyed; the military strength of the late victors had proved a broken sword. For nations unwilling and, in a practical political sense, unable to take the ever more enormous risks of modern war, the hypothecation of their military strength as a basis of exchange in international relations was no longer feasible.

Even for Hitler, who was both willing and able to take greater risks than the Western allies, it was to prove infeasible in the end. He equipped himself with the armaments, and adopted basically the same methods of military threat which had failed to preserve Franco-British power in order to make himself the dominant power in Europe. He probably both intended and expected to do so without actual war, or at most without more than "limited" war, like that with which he erased Poland. Hitler was a superb master of what John Foster Dulles later taught us to call "brinkmanship," and he nearly got away with it (as Dulles never did). He was also a true exponent of what is now called "deterrence." He would deter the superdestructive general war—with the memory of 1918 vividly in his mind, he was always fearful of the "two-front war"—and hoped to avoid it while attaining his ends by lesser means. Except for the savagery and brutality with which it was expressed, Hitler's basic international policy was quite close to that now advanced, in polite and (of course) moralistic terms, by the Kennedy Administration's strategists of "deterrence" and "limited-war capabilities." Initially, he was brilliantly successful. But in the end it did not work. Another decade passed. Ten years after the reoccupation of the Rhineland in 1936, a macabre scene in the bomb-cellars under the ruins of his Reichs Chancellery demonstrated that the war system was as useless to him as it had been to his opponents. By reviving it, he had destroyed the Versailles solution, but had put nothing in its place, and had only ruined Germany in the process, as well as destroying himself.

The war system—that is to say, the adjustment of international power relations by military threat and resort to organized international war—was an anachronism by the end of the First World War; with the appearance of the nuclear weaponry at the end of the Second it became totally unworkable. This was not, of course, immediately apparent. Indeed, there is some reason to suggest that it was only the appearance of the atomic bomb which saved the war system from the contradictions which would have been even more evident in 1945 if the immolation of Hiroshima and Nagasaki had never taken place. "Air power," which had been regarded through five terrible years as the ultimate determinant of human history, came in for disconcerting re-examination. While its random horror and destructiveness (as well as its enormous expense) were beyond question, its actual effects, both on military success and on the national policies and purposes which victory was supposed to serve, seemed to have been disproportionately small and dangerously erratic. The enormity, and underlying futility, of the total agony might, as in 1918, have led to serious question about the whole international system of which it was a consequence. But with the atomic bomb, air "power" was suddenly magnified by a factor of 2,000. Here was the "absolute weapon." If military power had proved an inefficient instrument for solving the real problems of the world of 1939, now here at last was a weapon big enough to solve any and all problems. The war system was again in business.

Or so, at first, it seemed. The opposite was of course the truth. The new weapons were too powerful. They were too powerful to be employed in actual war with any hope of achieving any useful results thereby; they were too powerful to be hypothecated as the base for a diplomacy of threat and brinkmanship. It was as impossible to change the "power" of a multimegaton thermonuclear bomb into usable political or social values as it would be to change a $1,000 bill in a country drugstore on a Sunday—as both Dulles with his "massive retaliation" and Khrushchev with his not infrequent "bomb-rattling" were to discover. To operate the system of international power relationships on the basis of military threats and balances had become impracticable, and in fact the system has not been so operated since 1945. In the sixteen years since the explosion over Hiroshima, there have been many "deadly quarrels" (in Richardson's phrase) and localized wars; but the

28

The Uselessness of Military Power

Sino-American war in Korea, resulting from the Korean "police action," is the only example of large-scale, organized international conflict of this period, and that was of the "limited" variety, which ended in stalemate. And while threats of war and extermination have been frequent, they have not been controlling—they have hardly even been influential—in the development of the politics and power relationships of the era.

There is no evidence whatever to indicate that the American atomic monopoly, prior to 1949, prevented a Soviet military conquest of Western Europe; just as there is no evidence to indicate that Soviet superiority in conventional armaments prevented a Western onslaught upon the Soviet Union. There is, indeed, nothing to suggest that Moscow, any more than Washington, has ever contemplated a revival of the war system, in the manner of Hitler, Mussolini, and the Japanese militarists; and international history since 1945 is of a strikingly different character from that of the late twenties and thirties. The Soviet-Western competition in armaments, unlike that initiated by Hitler, has in fact been defensive on both sides; the huge arsenals have not been deployed behind specific agressive political ends. The Russians, like John Foster Dulles, have not hesitated to threaten "massive retaliation"—as in the Suez crisis, over Cuba, over Berlin, and in more general terms—but it has always been "retaliation" only, and seems to have had hardly more influence over events than did the Dulles policy. The cold war has proceeded along quite different lines from those of Hitler's cold war on the Versailles system.

The Communist onslaught on South Korea in 1950 might be cited against this conclusion, but since almost nothing is known about its motivation or the political and military circumstances surrounding it, it is not a convincing example. The Russians presumably authorized this military adventure in what looked like a local situation; but we do not even know that it was they who incited it, or, if so, for what reasons. It seems quite certain that they did not intend to initiate a major trial of military strength; they did nothing of consequence to avert the defeat of the North Koreans, which was practically complete by November, 1950; and after the intervention of the Chinese had reversed the military situation, they used their influence to bring the "new war" to an end on the original lines. The "cold war"—a misnomer from the beginning—has not in fact been waged by military means or direct military threats; it has, indeed, turned upon two great issues, neither of which is susceptible to resolution by military means.

These basic issues, while closely intertwined, are not the same. The first deals with the past: it involves the liquidation of the Second World War and the rebuilding, out of the ruined and fragmented world of 1945, of a reasonably stable international power structure, a reasonably viable system for the organization of men. The second basic problem deals with the future: it involves a great-power competition, if not for control of, at least for influence over, the vast revolutionary process now sweeping the underdeveloped peoples of Asia, Africa, and Latin America. To neither of these fundamental problems is the old system of military power, military threat, and aggression really relevant. It should be obvious that one cannot repair the cataclysmic dislocations left behind by one great war through starting another one. It should be almost as obvious that a competition for influence over a great revolutionary process cannot be carried on successfully by military threat and great-power war. Korea offers an example. The divided Korea of 1950 was a direct legacy of the Second War and contained within it all the instabilities which that struggle had generated; the Korea of today, divided between two totalitarian dictatorships, one Communist and one military, is not a legacy from the past but one symbol (however ugly) of a hopefully more stable future. Whatever happens to the two Koreas, there is, I believe, little likelihood that their relations will be settled by organized war, and, even should this happen, almost none that the Koreans will drag the great powers into a major conflict.

The struggle to liquidate the Second War has been long, arduous, and frequently dangerous. There is, I submit, reason to believe that it is approaching its end. Through many difficult crises — in Finland, in Iran, in Greece, in Austria, in Czechoslovakia (and, one must add, in Hungary), in Korea—the great-power quarrel has been moving rather steadily toward settlement. It has not always seemed to be settlement with justice, but it has been settlement with increasing stability. And in the aftermath of a global war, stability is more important (and conceivably may even be more "just") than a perfect justice. The European and great-power structure which emerged after 1918 was highly unstable, and every attempt to balance it by rearmament and military threat and counterthreat rendered it only more so, until a second collapse became inevitable. The great-power system today is far better ballasted. It is framed around three great modes of power organization—the Chinese Communist state, the Russian Communist empire, and the Western democratic-capitalist alliance. Each has in large measure stabilized its internal political, economic, and territorial relations; in all, the peoples seem substantially to have accepted the governance under which they live, and even along most of the vast frontiers which separate them, one does not find the aggravated irredentist nationalisms which wrecked the system of Versailles. There seems to be little likelihood of revolution within any of them—certainly the Russian, like the Western, system is intensely conservative so far as its own affairs are concerned, and the same is probably increasingly true of the Chinese system. Each of the three major systems is in practice recognized by the others as essentially indestructible for the foreseeable future. Each has become, for the other two, an established fact of international life; each is the product of forces now irreversible; and each presents a viable and creative mode for organizing the activities of men. They must either make peace or make a war in which all systems are certain to perish. This is not a bad foundation for peace-making.

In the liquidation of the Second World War there appear to remain but two major (and admittedly very dangerous) items of unfinished business: the German Question and the Chinese Question symbolized in the problem of Formosa. The position in Germany is obviously anomalous as well as unstable; and one cannot help feeling that Khrushchev is well justified in forcing it to a solution which will recognize the existing facts and power positions. There is good reason for compelling the West to fish or cut bait. Whether the coarseness of his methods will end in eviscerating the negotiation he offers and precipitating the war which he wants no more than anyone else is perhaps a grim question; but at least for the first time since 1945 a reasonably lasting settlement of the German and Central European positions appears to have entered the realm of the possible, for the West as well as for the Russians. And the military gestures being made by both sides can hardly conceal the situation. Patently futile as preparations for war, they are little more than (very expensive) "media of communication" —ways of letting the other side know one's intent. They are also inefficient for the purpose, and may go wrong. If not, the final liquidation of the Second World War in Europe should be achieved. And its liquidation in East Asia should not then be impossible. The result will be a reasonable stabilization of the great-power system, to which military power and military threat will thereafter be more or less irrelevant.

There remains the great-power competition for beneficial interest in and influence over the continuing revolution in Asia, Africa, and Latin America. To imagine that this immense revolutionary phenomenon can be controlled or channeled in any significant way by war between the major military powers is completely to misunderstand its complex character; while to describe it in terms of a "war"—cold or hot—between the USSR and the United States is to reveal an egotistic paucity of insight into the needs and aspirations of the peoples involved, and the intricate power relationships it presents, that rivals the blindest demagoguery of an African nationalist or Communist theoretician. The competition between the Soviet Union and the West (China should probably be included as a third party, though the Chinese position is still obscure) for commanding influence in the revolutionary process is real and perhaps of considerable ultimate significance; but it is not a war, and military considerations are almost wholly irrelevant to it.

The Communist conquest of China, culminating in 1949, cannot be described as a "war," even a vicarious one, between the United States and the Soviet Union. Each of the two great powers, it is true, lent military aid and other support to the side which it favored, but the outcome was in no sense determined by the amount or degree of this outside intervention. Despite its greatly superior military potential, the United States could not have "saved" China, even if it had had reason or stomach for making the attempt. The forces which led to the communization of China were simply beyond control or significant influence by outside military might; and even the civil war itself was much more a political than a military phenomenon. The expansion of Soviet influence in Cuba was not a consequence of military factors and has not, in fact, materially affected the great-power military position. *Fidelismo* did not triumph in Cuba because of Soviet military power, while all the preponderant military power of the United States has been impotent to reverse the situation. Similarly, the Soviet Union saw no way in which to bring its military power to bear to dictate the outcome of the struggle in the Congo among the pro-Communist heirs to Lumumba, the pro-Western regime in Katanga, and the African neutralists who appear to be in control of the federal government.

The Kennedy Administration's new enthusiasm for adding a "limited-war capability" to the "deterrent" is a tacit—perhaps unconscious—admission of the uselessness of military power and organized war as a basis for great-power relationships. Similarly, the Pentagon's sudden interest in guerrilla and "psychological" warfare is an admission of the uselessness of formal war in the competition for influence over the "revolution of expectations." The corridors of the Pentagon are suddenly full of students of the military works of Mao Tse-tung, of the French military theorists of "pacification" and guerrilla war, and of technical studies of the operations of such revolutionary forces as the Algerian Army of National Liberation. These studies have produced a good deal of rather naïve thinking — exemplified, perhaps, in the abortive emigré descent on Cuba —but they do show a new understanding of the limitations on military action in dealing with the great-power competition over the "revolution of expectations." While the revolution has proceeded so far with a rather surprisingly small amount of bloodshed, violence will no doubt continue to recur. Where it does, it will almost certainly fall into these patterns of civil and guerrilla war, "psychological" conflict, mob action, virulent propaganda, and silent populist resistance, rather than into those of formally organized war appropriate to the politico-military relations of the major military powers. And to the extent to which the great powers fall afoul of each other in their competition for influence in the revolutionary process, they will use these indirect and irregular instrumentalities of force, rather than organized war, to resolve their issues. For in this area, none other are applicable.

Even where indirect violence of this kind may enter into the great-power competition—along with the more significant instrumentalities of political and economic support, propagandist and "infiltrative" activities—the competition will not be a war and will not have the consequences for the international power structure usually associated with formal wars. The appearance of a Communist-type dictatorship in a new nation, strongly backed by Moscow, does not automatically add that nation to the Russian power complex, or even to a more vaguely imagined "Communist power." Even where the new leaders are most strongly influenced by Russian (or Chinese) Communism, they are usually nationalists first and Communists only second, if at all. Many who, like Nasser, have utilized Russian help and imitated many of the Communist methods in their struggles to power, have, on achieving success, proved to be anything but agents of Moscow or even of Communist dogma. The oft-repeated prediction that unless the Western democratic capitalist states maintain their *military* defenses (which are irrelevant in this context) Communism will sweep the globe, leaving Western Europe and North America as a helpless island of freedom in a world of Communist totalitarian oppression, seems a fantastic distortion, corresponding in no way with the most plainly visible facts of the present situation.

The Russians have never, so far as I am aware, announced the "domination of the world" as their goal. They do, of course, endlessly repeat their prediction of an ultimately inevitable global triumph of Communism, and indicate their intention to assist this ineluctable process by all available means—among which they do not, either in theory or in practice, include organized war or military aggression. Their great military establishments exist, in practice as well as in theory, to defend the process against reversal by an allegedly aggressive capitalism; but as a means of promoting it, organized war is considered to be useless if not self-defeating. The result is the essentially nonmilitary competition for influence in the revolution. In the face of what is actually going on, one would have to be a dogmatic Communist to believe that the *inevitable* result must be the triumph of thoroughgoing Communist dictatorship everywhere in the world, or even everywhere outside of Western Europe and North America.

The revolution of expectations is a highly complex phenomenon, defying any simplistic analysis—whether Western or Communist—and any broad and simple over-all policy concepts applied to it. To see it as a mere black-and-white "struggle between Communism and democracy" is to be grotesquely myopic, a victim of an outworn and now grossly inadequate symbolism. It does, to be sure, involve a power "struggle," but one far more intricate, various, and confused than the simple notion of "Communism versus democracy" can possibly encompass. Basically, no doubt, this is a revolution against the immemorial conditions of poverty and privation imposed upon the "mass" by the agrarian-feudal societies of the past and still imposed by their successors in the vast underdeveloped areas today. It thus represents a revolutionary economic demand for industrialization, and a revolutionary political demand for the overthrow of the feudalistic social systems which have in general denied to the masses participation in the rewards of modern technology. But if it is simple in these broad outlines, it is inordinately complex in the power conflicts to which these give rise. Wherever it appears in force, the revolution requires revision—and often drastic revision—of established class structures, productive and distributive patterns, patterns of vested interest, of political control, of colonial or international relationship. In all these revisions complex power issues are involved, ranging all the way from issues over the power of the tribal chieftains in the new African republics to the power of the Soviet Union on the world stage vis-à-vis Western capitalistic democracy.

If Russian Communist "infiltration" has achieved some success in the competition for influence over these processes, it is certainly not because of Soviet military might. But neither is it primarily because of the superior appeal of Marxist-Leninist theology,[2] nor even because of the demonstrated ability of the

---

[2] Any more than Moslem theology explains the rise of the Negro Muslims in the United States.

Russian Communist system (and now perhaps of the Chinese) to effect the rapid industrialization of an underdeveloped people. Such things are but parts of a complex which can be best understood, I believe, by saying that in many situations populist totalitarian dictatorship in general and Russian Communism in particular have offered a more efficient, or at least a more workable, means of organizing the intricate power relationships involved than has anything in the gift of Western capitalistic democracy.

In the competition for influence over the revolutionary process, the Communists enjoy certain obvious advantages. In the first place, conservative though they now are at home, they are themselves the products of just this kind of revolution, and are adept in its requirements. The new Russian imperialism is unburdened by the commitments to colonialism which still hang around the necks of the nineteenth-century imperial powers. The West often manifests a kind of hurt surprise over the fact that the new, intensely nationalistic regimes do not manifest the same angry fear and resentment over Russian imperial expansion that they direct toward the old colonial powers. But this is to overlook the fact that whereas Western colonialism was imposed by force of arms from without, Soviet expansion has operated consistently through indigenous leaders and movements.

The Russian Communists are unworried by the old rules of the international power game, and they can offer the new aspirants in the power struggle techniques of violence, infiltration, and control which are more practically useful to them than democratic ideology or democratic political processes. Uncommitted to colonial groups (as was France in Algeria), they are equally uncommitted to domestic property rights and capital; they can back Castro's confiscation of American and other foreign capital with a *sang froid* which no American government could manifest, even though it had decided (as conceivably it might) that the confiscation was in the long-run interests of international order. All these are very powerful advantages in the competition for control of the revolution. Yet they are accompanied by drawbacks of their own, and they are clearly not decisive, for the revolution of expectations has not everywhere (and not even predominantly, outside of China) fallen into the mold of Russian Communism.

India, after China the greatest of the underdeveloped countries, has managed to meet her unusually difficult power problems within the form of a reasonably democratic government. While one-party populist dictatorship seems pretty much to dominate the field elsewhere, it comes in a wide variety of forms and with a wide variety of solutions for the basic issues of agrarian reform, industrialization, and encrusted vested interest. Sometimes, as with Castro, the populist dictatorship is blatantly Communist in form; sometimes, as in many of the new African nations, it operates under rather thin veils of democratic process and a party system; sometimes, as in the interesting military dictatorships, it imitates neither Communism nor democracy, but seems to be trying to develop a new kind of workable elite-ism. In all these classifications one finds Western-oriented, Communist-oriented, and neutralist-oriented examples. To say that the inevitable result of Communist intervention in such a situation must be a totally communized world is to take a timidly narrow view of cause and effect in the political relationships of men; but to say that the result, whatever it may be, will be materially affected by the institutions of military defense and organized war is to border upon the absurd.

Such considerations lead to a conclusion directly opposite to Mr. Osgood's thesis that "the capacity to wage war" remains "an indispensable instrument of national survival" and welfare, because of the nature of contemporary international society and of Communist aims and strategy. It would, I contend, be truer to say that *because of the nature of contemporary international society and of Communist aims and strategy, the capacity to wage war is the most dispensable of all instruments of national survival and welfare;* and that unless it is somehow dispensed with there is not much hope for either welfare or survival. Real, effective national power on the modern world stage is no longer expressed accurately, if at all, by relative military strengths. It is interesting that those who seem best to understand the new Africa and to be most successful in dealing with its complexities are neither the superarmed Russians nor the superarmed Americans but the Israelis—whose military strength does not extend beyond the Levant. The great military establishments which exist are not practically usable in the conduct of international relations, and in general are not being so used today; and if it were possible to rid ourselves of the whole apparatus—the armaments, the military establishments, and the war system they embody—international relations could be conducted far more safely, more efficiently, and more creatively in face of the staggering real problems facing humankind than is now the case.

Will this ever be possible? Quite obviously it cannot be done today or tomorrow; but we are already far beyond the point where one can say that it is demonstrably impossible— indeed, a more persuasive case can already be made for the contention that the demilitarization of the international order is ultimately inevitable. The necessity is already so evident that we have created a new Federal agency charged (in effect, if not quite in so many words) with the task of bringing it about. One may doubt that it will make much progress, for "disarmament" in and of itself is no more hopeful as a solution today than it was in 1898. It offers at most a technical means of building upon political, diplomatic, and psychological foundations which have yet to be firmly laid. But the appearance of the new agency is itself one of many signs that they are being laid, and one may hope that the process will continue.

If it is to do so, the first requisite is that responsible statesmanship in all the great military powers should discard, or at least mute, the dogmatic myths and fantasies with which they becloud the world, in order to face the clear facts of the international power structure. We are accustomed to think of the Communists as the outstanding victims of their mystical doctrine; to me, it seems that the West is, if anything, more densely blinded by its own doctrinaire misconceptions of reality. This is almost certainly true of Western statesmen, who, however clearly they may themselves see, are hampered by difficulties of participational democracy and uncontrolled mass media of opinion with which their Communist counterparts do not have to contend. We would like, if we could, to exclude patently meaningless phrases like "the imperialist aggressors" from the

Communist vocabulary; the least we might do ourselves is to exclude phrases like "the cold war" from our own discussion of problems to which they are simply inapplicable.

Certainly the West, no less than the Russians and the Chinese, must bring itself to accept the irreversible verdicts of the Second World War and its aftermath. The West must bring itself to agree to a reasonably stable settlement, in accord with the new power positions which have been established. Specifically, I believe that this means it must accept the partition of Germany and the stabilization of the Communist satellite system in Central Europe, including East Germany. With that much, West Berlin should be negotiable; without it, the West might as well stop talking about negotiation. The existing power position simply allows of no further latitude.

It may be objected that "the existing power position" means the existing *military* power position; and that to use the concept vitiates the whole argument as to the inutility of military power in international relations. I do not think this necessarily follows. Unlike Hitler, Khrushchev has not deployed his military might as a means of forcing a settlement; he has threatened only to use it should the West deploy its military power to overturn a solution which all the nonmilitary power factors involved seem to him to render necessary and essential. It is the deepest source of the West's embarrassment that it cannot do this, any more than it could do so in a demilitarized world. One might ask what the outcome would be in a state of universal demilitarization. The West could not prevent Khrushchev from signing his treaty with East Germany; would it have a worse or a better chance of getting reasonable guarantees for the retention of West Berlin as a part of the West German political and economic system? The existing military systems on both sides can end by precipitating a wholly useless (and probably catastrophic) war, but they cannot alter the larger power relationships which, if there is to be no war, point emphatically toward a settlement in general along the lines Khrushchev proposes.

If the Second World War can be successfully liquidated without a Third, the world will then proceed to the problems of "peaceful co-existence" in a revolutionary and fluid world power situation. To the solution of these problems, organized military power on the present colossal scale will be irrelevant, and will increasingly be understood to be so. It does not seem absurd to hope that in this situation the giant arsenals will begin to atrophy, and that proposals for mutual reduction and elimination of armaments will enter the realm of practical international politics. This should happen, unless the arsenals should explode of themselves under the appalling charges of fear and terror being build into them.

It is to this frightful prospect that the present students of "arms control" are devoting their attention. Their immediate object is not to eliminate or necessarily even to reduce existing armaments but to achieve a maximum degree of stability, to "balance" the weapons and weapons systems of the various military powers in such a way as to minimize the possibility of their exploding. I think one must respect their arguments. Certainly, it is difficult to see any present possibility of "general and complete disarmament" of the kind put forward by Khrushchev; and until one can, attempts at stabilization of the great military systems are far more important than attempts to eliminate them. My difficulty with the theorists of arms control is that their policies—based as they are on the assumption that war (of some kind) is ineradicable as the base for international relations, and that the war system (expressed as "the capacity to wage war") is indispensable to national survival and welfare —are likely to prove as self-defeating in the end as all previous approaches to disarmament.

Put in its simplest (but I do not think oversimplified) terms, these policies call for a balance of the great nuclear deterrents that will prevent their use—except as deterrents— and so remove them from the international power complex. But since the complex is conceived of as being inherently military, and the exercise of power through military threat and war is considered ineradicable from international society, various forms and degrees of "limited war" capabilities must be introduced to settle the power issues which, under this view, could no longer be settled by resort to the nuclear arsenals. But, moderate and pacific as these views certainly are, they represent (as has already been suggested) an analysis of the international power complex no different in its theoretic fundamentals from that which Adolf Hitler applied to the world of the early thirties. We will deter the catastrophic great war by balancing the big military establishments, but use more "limited" military threats and wars to achieve all the ends, defensive or otherwise, which seem to us "vital." This seems to me a form of having one's cake and eating it, too, which in the long run is bound to lead to the same kind of catastrophe (this time enormously magnified) to which it led Hitler and, with him, the Western world.

Mr. Osgood uses phrases which I find baffling. He speaks of "the nonviolent uses of military power," "the offensive and defensive exploitation of military power by means short of war," "the political and psychological exploitation of military power," and so on. The "nonviolent" use of "military power" is to me a contradiction in terms. If it is not, then I think we would have to admit Hitler's successful partition of Czechoslovakia in 1938, without a war, as an instance of the nonviolent exploitation of military power. So long as we reserve to ourselves the right to engage in such uses of military power, even though we hope and intend to confine them to limited-war forms, it seems to me that we are making the ultimate total disaster as inevitable as it was made by Hitler.

I contend that there is no rational military policy for the United States except a policy which begins with the explicit and avowed objective of attaining general and complete disarmament, a demilitarized world, and an abolition of the war system and the vast apparatus of terror which has grown up around it. No other policy, however ingeniously devised, seems to me to hold out any hope of insuring the security, to say nothing of the continued welfare, of the American people.

It is not suggested that a policy so based could be easily or promptly brought to fruition. It is not suggested that the United States should immediately and unilaterally divest itself of its nuclear arsenals and other military defenses. While a good theoretical case can be made for the proposition that a unilateral divestiture of this kind would in fact redound more to the real security and welfare of the American people than any other course, the time has not come when it would be humanly possible to translate theory into practice. For the present, we will have to make do with a war system balanced as stably and safely as is possible. What is suggested is that we are already entering a period which makes the demilitarized world a political possibility, for the first time in the history of international organization. But the possibility cannot be realized unless all our military and defense policies are consciously directed toward its realization. If they are, there are great possibilities for advance. Unless they are, there seems little possibility of any end result save nuclear extermination.

Herman Kahn

•

STRATEGY, FOREIGN POLICY, AND THERMONUCLEAR WAR

In a rapidly changing and unfamiliar situation—such as the relationships between deterrence, defense, and modern technology—simple conceptual "models" are often more useful than undisciplined intuition in discussing and guiding policy. Of course, even the best models can be so oversimplified as to be useless or misleading. There is, however, no reason to believe that relatively sophisticated models are more likely to be misleading than the simpler models and analogies frequently used as an aid to judgment. This paper will therefore consider several conceptual models involving some aspects of the use and control of nuclear war.

The word *use* is deliberately chosen to emphasize the paradox that today we preserve the peace by threat of war. Americans often tend to forget that the threat of war can be credible only if a war could occur. When we deter the Soviets by the threat that if they provoke us in a limited war, subsequent reprisals may blow up into an all-out thermonuclear war, we are deliberately or inadvertently *using* the threat, and therefore the possibility, of nuclear war. When we tell our allies that our Strategic Air Command protects them from Soviet aggression, we are in a sense *using* nuclear war.

This deliberate terminology may arouse animosity from both the "Right" and the "Left." The Right, often wishing to stand firm, does not like the reasonably correct implication that if we deliberately accept .01 chance of killing 100,000,000 people we have in a probabilistic sense "killed" 1,000,000 people, which itself raises several moral issues.[1] The Left tends not to like the implication of acceptability and necessity in the word *use*. Either of the above objections could be correct. Perhaps we should use war, but not mention, discuss, or analyze this use. Perhaps we should do all these things privately, but not publicly. I do not know whether any or all of these propositions are right or wrong, but I think they are wrong.

In any case, we have procured nuclear equipment and intend to maintain it, unless and until better arrangements can be worked out. We should understand that these actions necessarily imply a possibility of both deliberate and inadvertent thermonuclear war. It would be every bit as irresponsible to ignore the resulting risks as it would be to overstate them deliberately in the hope of influencing policy through persuasive but incorrect arguments.

WHERE WE HAVE BEEN—A BRIEF HISTORICAL REVIEW

1945–1955

A simple model seemed appropriate in the late forties and early fifties. The United States had an effective monopoly of nuclear weapons. It could therefore threaten the Soviets with massive damage should they engage in provocations, while they could do little or nothing in reprisal. Therefore, many concluded that the

---

1

		Some Awkward Choices		
Policy	Probability of Loss	Amount of Loss	Expected Loss	Probability of No Loss
A	1.0	$3,000	$3,000	0
B	.1	$300,000	$30,000	.9
C	.01	$30,000,000	$300,000	.99
D	.001	$3,000,000,000	$3,000,000	.999

If a decision-maker were to have to choose between the four policies indicated above, he is very likely to have the preferences A, B, C, D. If, however, lives are at stake rather than dollars and if the decision-maker is going to have to acknowledge responsibility for any deaths which result from his choice (and the operation of chance), then his preferences are likely to be reversed; for example, most decision-makers would choose C over A, because under policy C there are ninety-nine chances out of a hundred of the policy being successful and only one chance out of a hundred of a failure, while A is guaranteed to fail. True the expected loss under policy C is greater, but it is a risk, not a certainty, and in most cases some judicious wishful thinking will partially conceal both the degree and consequence of the risk.

Soviets, being rational and prudent, would be deterred from any but the most minor provocations.

Though we did not realize it, there were many things wrong with this picture. First, United States capability was exaggerated. There is now serious doubt that during the later forties and early fifties we could have done as much damage to a Soviet war effort as the Germans did during the Second World War by their occupation of the most highly industrialized and productive portion of the Soviet Union. Second, the enormity of nuclear weapons tended to make them unusable by a nation with our attitudes, traditions, and morals. Although we used such weapons on a relatively minor scale at the end of the Second World War, this came at the end of a major war, not at the beginning of a relatively minor conflict. Furthermore, even Hiroshima and Nagasaki were becoming uncomfortable subjects for some Americans. Third, deterrence is a psychological phenomenon, and it now seems likely that Stalin underestimated the potentiality of the nuclear weapons we did have. Last, but by no means least, Western Europe, a vast and immensely valuable hostage, lay almost defenseless before the Soviet Union. The Soviets could and did deter us by threatening Europe.

It was therefore by no means certain that a United States capability to win or punish actually did deter the Soviets. Nor is it completely clear that the United States actually had that capability, or even that, if it did, the victory would be worth the cost to us and our allies. One can conjecture today that the main reasons for the comparative caution exercised by the Soviets from 1945 to 1955 were fear of United States mobilization potential, fear of revolt by a war-weary people, a major preoccupation with Soviet reconstruction, and possibly even a feeling of indigestion with the satellites and a corresponding lack of desire to gobble up more.

1955–1960

By the middle fifties the simple view of United States strategic superiority was replaced in much of the literature by another equally simple one. In this model the Soviets had created a deterrent which countered and negated our deterrent, thus giving rise to an automatic, symmetrical, and reliable balance of terror. There were varying beliefs as to the stability of the balance of terror. Many believed it to be an effective deterrent against all deliberate attacks because of the disaster to the attacker which would follow inevitably.

Surprisingly large numbers of both laymen and experts believed that any and all thermonuclear wars would automatically mean not only mutual annihilation, but very likely the end of all human life. These views came from different sources. Some came from the totally uninformed; some resulted from an understandable emotional reaction to estimates of the damage that could result from the direct effects of nuclear weapons, or such indirect agents as carbon-14 or strontium-90; and some were due simply to a failure to distinguish between an unhappily large number of casualties and a total, universal doom.

Others held more modest views as to the probable result of a war. Most of these still believed that the immediate damage would inevitably be so large that no rational decision-maker would ever actually initiate such a war. Even those who thought it possible that something like victory might be achieved by one side or the other in some circumstances, also felt that the uncertainties were so great that, even with the most optimistic paper plans, no rational decision-maker would ever initiate a war. For these and other reasons, almost all analysts and thoughtful people believed in the existence of a firm balance of terror so far as deliberate attack was concerned in spite of the fact that the Soviets had a relatively ineffective intercontinental capability (because of both operational incompetency and inadequate equipment) while the United States appeared to have (on paper) a disarming first-strike capability during most of this period. Once again, United States moral and political inhibitions, Soviet caution in provoking the United States, and the European hostage may have combined to play as big a role in the Soviet capability for deterrence as their relatively small and unreliable second-strike capability.

In the middle fifties there was amazingly little discussion of the possibility of inadvertent violation. With the advent of alert and ready missiles and bombers, however, when split-second timing became crucial, there came an increasing sophistication among knowledgeable people concerning the details, complexities, and possible failures of military systems. It was then that inadvertent war began to be discussed more widely. Many experts now believe that the possibility of inadvertent war is the central problem of the sixties, and possibly the seventies.

Once the firm belief in the balance of terror became widely held, some experts began to think that the nuclear weapons had cancelled each other out, and that the military situation had become similar to the prenuclear age. The experience of Korea and Indochina seemed to bear out the view that we were back to the exclusive use of old-fashioned high explosives for the waging of war. Soon, however, more complicated notions began to appear. First came the idea that nuclear weapons could be useful tactically as a weapon against large masses of troops and equipment during a small-scale war. Since the all-out use of nuclear weapons was equated with automatic mutual annihilation, it was felt that a limited use would continue limited and would not lead to a disastrous all-out war.

By 1957 when the most influential treatise[2] advocating the use of tactical nuclear weapons had appeared, the notion that these weapons were or should be "conventional" already had begun to lose favor among many professional military planners and civilian analysts. These people pointed out persuasively that with no obvious boundary lines to distinguish the "large" from the "small" use of nuclear weapons, there could be no reliable way for the two combatants to agree explicitly or implicitly on a natural boundary. It then came to be felt that the one and only rule on which two angry but prudent contestants might agree would be the rule not to use nuclear weapons at all. Many of those who felt that this convention was not the only feasible one, still recognized it as a valuable, and perhaps the best, line that could be drawn because "agreements" higher on the nuclear scale would be both dangerous and unreliable. Thus, almost all theorists came eventually to believe that limited wars should be fought only with high explosives.

As early as 1955, Professor Leo Szilard seriously suggested the possibility of a form of limited use of strategic forces: retaliation to extreme provocation by initiating punishment exempli-

[2] Henry Kissinger, *Nuclear Weapons and Foreign Policy* (New York: Council on Foreign Relations, 1957).

fied in tit-for-tat city exchanges.[3] A few years later, writers such as Morton Kaplan and Thomas Schelling,[4] without advocating Szilard's exact suggestion, emphasized the possible use of nuclear threats or actual explosions in "bargaining." They paid serious analytical attention to the possible use of two specific forms of limited nuclear war: One is what I have called Controlled Reprisal but which is often referred to as limited strategic retaliation. The other is the thermonuclear show of force.

A Controlled Reprisal is a limited nuclear attack upon a target such as a city or other valuable property in reprisal for some serious provocation. It can be thought of as a nuclear deterrent by the threat of less than an all-out attack. The thermonuclear show of force is not so much an attack as a vivid demonstration that should some provocation not stop, there is a serious danger of escalation into a large (but possibly still controlled) thermonuclear war. In a Controlled Reprisal or thermonuclear show of force one is not so much forcing one's will on the enemy as a direct result of the military operations, but is either inflicting a very controlled punishment for some provocation, or making a demonstration of resolve, or both. These current and somewhat bizarre-sounding concepts have been extensively discussed. They now appear less bizarre than they seemed at first not because their nature has changed but as a logical consequence of the bizarreness of the balance of terror as the major method of maintaining peace and resolving conflicts.[5]

Such actions could be taken by either side. If, for example, there were an uprising in East Germany and the West Germans sent troops to support it, the Soviets might use a single high-altitude nuclear burst over Western Europe or the United States. Such an action would demonstrate more clearly than any threats or ultimatums that the Soviets would go far indeed to prevent a successful invasion of East Germany. In other words, when a nation has used one thermonuclear weapon, it becomes much more credible that it is prepared to use many. It would

[3] Leo Szilard, "Disarmament and the Problem of Peace," *Bulletin of the Atomic Scientists*, XI, No. 8 (October 1955), pp. 297–307.

[4] Morton Kaplan, "The Calculus of Nuclear Deterrence," *World Politics*, XI (October 1958), pp. 20–43; Thomas C. Schelling, *The Strategy of Conflict* (Cambridge, Mass.: Harvard University Press, 1960).

[5] See Klaus Knorr (ed.), *Limiting Strategic War: Essays on Nuclear Strategy* (New York: Praeger, 1962).

then be up to us to back down or negotiate. Alternatively we could threaten retaliation in kind with all the worries of escalation that such retaliation would bring, or even deliberately escalate by using more or larger weapons in our counterdemonstration. It is precisely because there seems to be no natural dividing line, once nuclear weapons have been used to cause actual destruction, that even the symbolic use of a single nuclear weapon is frightening. In effect, one side is saying to the other, "You had better back down, because I will not." This is a variation of the well-known game of "chicken."

These concepts were developed largely on the assumption of a firm balance of terror, with experts investigating its effects on a world in which all-out war had been banned but no rule of law substituted. At about this time, however, the belief in the reality of the stable balance of terror came under heavy attack on two separate fronts. First, the idea developed that a nation initiating the first nuclear strike had an enormous advantage, because the nation that was struck might find its ability to strike back (second-strike capability) small compared to its first-strike capability.[6] In addition to noticing the important distinction between a first-strike and a second-strike capability, investigators began to notice that, destructive as the use of nuclear weapons against civil society would be, the destruction need not be as total as some had thought. The difference was not that the strategic forces were completely vulnerable or that the civilian societies were invulnerable. It was a question of degree. Strategic forces were not as invulnerable as had been widely supposed and civil societies were less vulnerable.

Once the advantage of the first strike began to be understood, there were some who went too far and did not realize that the relative advantages of the first and second strike were largely a matter of significant degree. They compared the situation to the old-fashioned Western gun duel. In this model, the man who drew first not only had the upper hand, but usually got away scot-free; there was no advantage at all in waiting if one were sure to win. Such a situation is unstable, indeed. A mere suspicion of the other side could set off a "pre-emptive"

[6] See Albert Wohlstetter, "The Delicate Balance of Terror," *Foreign Affairs*, XXXVII (January 1959), pp. 211–34.

strike. However, even among those who did not go to this extreme, great interest developed in seeking so-called stable deterrence, a situation in which there would not be an enormous premium to either side in striking first. Interest in this subject was so great that a school grew up known as the Minimum Deterrence or Finite Deterrence group. They argued that the only possible purpose of strategic forces was effectively to negate, by threat of retaliation, the other side's strategic forces; having done that, nothing else would be needed or feasible in the strategic field. We would then have a stable and mutual balance of terror with no attempt to alleviate the consequences if deterrence failed. By and large, this view is now being rejected—at least so far as official United States policy is concerned.

WHERE WE ARE—CURRENT STRATEGIC CONCEPTS

I would like now to consider current United States policy. In many ways this policy is quite different from the views held by many sophisticated people in the late fifties, though like many avant-garde notions, it has many similarities with traditional concepts; indeed many feel that whatever changes have occurred in the last few years involve only nuances and not fundamentals. I will consider this "new" policy in terms of the objectives it seeks to fulfill.

It is useful to set forth the objectives explicitly at the outset. Modern technology, to a degree unprecedented in history, can provide weapons systems so highly specialized that an enthusiastic and competent but narrow-minded pursuit of one objective will not automatically result in meeting other objectives.

United States military policy currently seeks to achieve at least six broad strategic objectives:

1. *Type I Deterrence*—to deter a large attack on the military forces, population, or wealth of the United States, by threatening a high level of damage to the attacker in retaliation;

2. *Type II Deterrence*—to deter extremely provocative actions short of large attack on the United States (for example, a nuclear or even all-out conventional strike against Western Europe) by the threat of an "all-out" United States nuclear reprisal against the Soviet Union;

3. *Improved War Outcome*—to limit damage to United

States (and allied) population and wealth, and to improve the military outcome for the United States should a war occur;

4. *Stability*—to reduce the likelihood of an inadvertent thermonuclear war;

5. *Comprehensive Arms Control*—to control and limit both the arms race and the use of force in settling disputes;

6. *Type III Deterrence*—to deter provocations not covered by Type II Deterrence and provide support for the achievement of "peaceful" political objectives and for tactics such as Controlled Reprisal, other limited wars, mobilizations, negotiations, and so forth.

I do not propose to judge here the relative importance of these various objectives. During the past decade all of them have played major parts in the formation of United States defense policy. While they are to some extent competitive and inconsistent so far as over-all national security is concerned, they are also complementary; in most cases a catastrophic failure to achieve any one of them is unlikely to be rectified even by spectacular successes in the other five.

There are still other complications in designing and evaluating strategic forces. Not only may additional objectives come into being after a system has been built, but the balance among objectives may change. It is important, therefore, that our capability be flexible enough to accept efficiently increases, decreases, or major alterations in our objectives in reaction to changes in the technological, military, and political environment. Unless only a specialized question is being examined, studies of strategic forces must consider all six objectives jointly. Fortunately it often seems possible to design the components of our strategic forces to contribute to more than one of the objectives, and a well-designed strategic system will probably contribute a reasonable capability to all six.

Let us now consider each of these objectives and some of their implications in greater detail.

1. TYPE I DETERRENCE

Probably the most essential mission of our strategic forces is to deter deliberate direct attack on the United States (whether aimed primarily at military forces or cities) by influencing the enemy's calculations as to the relative advantages to himself of attacking or not attacking. We want the enemy's calculations, whether explicitly or implicitly made, to indicate clearly that in all circumstances an attack on the United States would be a serious mistake. It must distinctly appear that any attack, *however carefully designed or brilliantly executed,* will result in such a high probability of an unacceptable amount of damage being caused to some or all of the attacker's population, industry, or military forces, that our enemy must rule it out as a choice even if he is desperate or biased by wishful thinking.

Our ability to deter the Soviets depends on an estimate of what would be likely to happen if the Soviets were to strike *at a time and with tactics of their own choosing,* and we had to attempt to strike back with a *damaged* and perhaps *unco-ordinated* force which must operate in the *postattack environment.* The Soviets might attempt to follow up an attack with *threats to intimidate us into limiting our reprisal;* not only would Soviet active defenses be *completely alerted,* but if the strike had been preceded by a period of tension, they would probably have been *augmented* as well. Moreover their cities might be at least *partially evacuated.* Each of these factors increases considerably the difficulty of guaranteeing retaliation adequate to deter.

For this reason, the problem of assuring retaliation must be viewed as a whole. It is not enough to have large numbers of nuclear-weapon delivery-systems before an attack, or even enough to insure the survival of an adequate number of them after an attack. We must, in a sense, also assume the survival of a whole retaliatory system. We must protect the legal (presidential) decision-making machinery, vital military personnel, enough military command and control to execute an appropriate operation, and, finally, the resolution to carry out this operation.

Type I Deterrence is in part a psychological matter. It rests principally upon an enemy's judgment of the likelihood of various possible outcomes of an attack on the United States as compared to his nonthermonuclear war alternatives. Theoretically, if by some tricks we could convince the enemy that we had an invulnerable and overwhelming retaliatory power, we would not even need the hardware. Moreover, we might in at least one respect be better off, since nonexistent missiles will not go off accidentally. Unfortunately, in today's world we cannot rely on pulling off such a titanic bluff. We could not be certain or even very sure that the Soviets had not found us out. And unless we have faith in our deterrent we may be unwilling to so much as test it by standing firm in a crisis. Moreover, unless our own population was similarly fooled, internal pressures would prevent us from standing firm in any crisis. In all probability, the only way to convince all those who have to be convinced that we have a deterrent is actually to have one.

Our Type I Deterrent must, of course, do more than deter the most cautious and responsible Soviet decision-maker, who expects to win the cold war "peacefully," from risking all in an attack launched suddenly in cold blood. Our deterrent must be powerful enough to withstand all of the stresses and strains of the cold war, of sudden and unexpected crises, of possible accidents and miscalculations, of satellite revolts, of limited wars, of fanciful calculations by optimistic gamblers or simple-minded theoreticians, and of the tense situations in which "reciprocal fear of surprise attack" might destabilize an inadequate deterrent. We want it to be clear even to less responsible Soviet decision-makers that we have taken all of their most "optimistic" schemes into account.

Moreover, we want to deter the irrational and even the mad. It is sometimes stated that even an adequate Type I Deterrent would not deter an irrational enemy. This might be true if irrationality were an all-or-nothing matter. Actually, there are degrees of irrationality, and if the irrationality is sufficiently bizarre, the irrational decision-maker's subordinates are likely to step in. As a result, we should want a safety factor in Type I Deterrence systems so large as to impress even the irrational and irresponsible with the degree of their irrationality and therefore the need for caution. In short, a satisfactory Type I Deterrent for the United States must provide an objective basis for Soviet calculations that no matter how skillful, ingenious, or optimistic they are, and no matter how negatively they view their alternatives in a desperate crisis, an attack on the United States would entail a very high risk, indeed virtually guarantee an unacceptable large-scale destruction of Soviet civil society and military forces. As has been pointed out, such a Type I Deterrent may be difficult to achieve, because there are many possible asymmetries in thermonuclear war that could favor a decision to attack in a paper calculation and perhaps in the decision-maker's mind.

2. TYPE II DETERRENCE

One can distinguish at least three important deterrent situations, the first of which we have just described. The second, which we will call Type II Deterrence, is the deterrence of extremely provocative actions short of an attack upon the United States itself, by threat of a large attack on the Soviet Union. Although statements by the public officials are sometimes contradictory on this subject (e.g., nuclear war is unthinkable, but we will start one if the Soviets attack West Berlin), the United States does have solemn treaty obligations which, as these obligations are normally envisaged, could be honored in no other way. At some future date, the nonnuclear capability of NATO may be sufficient to repel a large but conventional attack on Western Europe. Until this time Western Europe will probably depend, at least in part, on Type II Deterrence (or Controlled Reprisal) to deter such attacks.

One basic distinction between Type I and Type II Deterrence is that Type I requires us to launch a counterattack after the enemy has launched an attack on our forces; Type II envisages a reprisal attack by our undamaged, and, at the moment, unthreatened forces. Although many people are willing to accept Type I Deterrence as being defensive, and therefore appropriate, they reject Type II Deterrence as bellicose, aggressive, or tending to stimulate the arms race. They handle the problems of Type II Deterrence either by denying they can arise, by advocating various lesser and seemingly safer responses, or by redefining Type II Deterrence as a kind of Type I Deterrence. A typical attitude is, "The Soviets will never attack Europe without attacking the United States first, or at the same time. It would be too dangerous for them" (i.e., the Type II Deterrence they do not wish to discuss will deter the Soviets successfully). Let us consider some of the possibilities, however.

As the acquisition of relatively invulnerable strategic capabilities by both sides proceeds, the balance of terror may grow firmer. The threat, or even the implied threat, of all-out war becomes less credible, hence less useful, as a deterrent. While it is by no means inevitable, one can easily imagine that by the late sixties or early seventies a reliable balance of terror between the Soviet Union and the United States could be achieved. Under these circumstances, the use by a rational (or at least rational-appearing) decision-maker of Type II Deterrence will not be feasible.

Many people believe that the same can be said of the early and mid-sixties. Although we can not now rely as much on the use of strategic threats as we could ten years ago, this does not mean there is no role for the strategic threat. All it means is that it plays a lesser role than it did in the recent past. This in turn means we must have more limited-war and other types of capabilities discussed under Type III Deterrence. But for the time being it is more a question of degree than of kind.

If we had no forces capable of Type II Deterrence and no possibility of an adequate level of Controlled Reprisal, the Soviets would know that they need not compromise in any crisis with one of our allies; they could achieve their goals merely by pressing hard enough. In such a case, we might take limited actions which would make their victory costly but not prohibitively so. It is easy to see what a bargaining advantage the Soviets would hold over our allies or neutrals. By pressing hard they might be able to achieve their goals painlessly. If, however, they guessed wrong and "went too far," they still would not suffer disaster, since, by assumption, we would not use our Strategic Air Command in reprisal. Our ally, however, would be risking total catastrophe at each step of the negotiations. The Soviets could even afford to be careless about getting into crises and staking a lot on "winning" them. In fact, a reputation for such carelessness would enhance their bargaining ability. In brief, then, if strategic forces are outmoded for Type II Deterrence objectives, we must develop new forces and policies until some more satisfactory and effective system of world order and security can be developed. Unsatisfactory and dangerous as Type II Deterrence may be, the interim measures may prove to be worse.

It is sometimes thought that the vulnerability of the United States forces is irrelevant to Type II Deterrence because in this case we would be attacking first. This is not correct. In order for Type II Deterrence to be effective, we would first have to possess a secure Type I Deterrent force. Otherwise an enemy might be tempted to pre-empt in any situation where he thought the use of Type II Deterrence likely or possible. Moreover, in order to use our Type II Deterrence effectively, we must also have a reasonably strong position in Improved War Outcome.[7] Only in such a case will our threat to attack be credible.

Another misconception concerning Type II Deterrence involves the distinction between active and passive deterrence. An active deterrent, as the name implies, requires an act of will on the part of the deterrer for the threat to be translated into action. In a passive deterrent the change from a contingent threat to an act is simply the result of an unthinking or unwilled response to the provocation. Many people regard Type I Deterrence as automatically passive and Type II Deterrence as necessarily active. Under current conditions, neither assumption may be completely valid.

In the first place, Type I Deterrence may not be so passive as is normally envisaged. If, for example, the Soviets destroyed a small number of initial strategic targets in the United States— say, a command and control headquarters—we would not know whether this had occurred by accident, through unauthorized behavior, as a Controlled Reprisal, or as a deliberate attempt to degrade our capability in order to pave the way for a full-scale attack. It would be difficult to imagine our reacting with an all-out attack. In this situation we might prefer to investigate, negotiate, or at most trade with the Soviets in some *quid pro quo* fashion, as in a Controlled Reprisal, and hope that this would discourage them from repeating their transgression. The handling of this type of situation should hardly be automatic.

Second, Type II Deterrence may exist in some degree even without an act of will. In some situations it may be completely unthinking. The kinds of provocative actions which the Soviets would have to take in order to justify our use of Type II Deterrence would in themselves automatically entail some risk of war by escalation, by accident, by miscalculation, by unauthorized behavior, or by sheer anger, without a really deliberative decision having been made. Therefore, a considerable, perhaps

---

[7] Discussed in the next section of this paper. (There are, of course, other reasons for wanting an Improved War Outcome capability.)

even sufficient, degree of Type II Deterrence might be obtained through such "passive" mechanisms.

Although the case for the sufficiency of passive measures to achieve either Type I or Type II Deterrence is plausible, it can be made too strongly; there are tactics available to the Soviets which they could explore and probe with relative safety if we had no military systems requiring an act of will on our part before they could be put into motion. The Soviets can teach us to be prudent. If our forces or our willingness to use them to achieve such deterrence objectives were sufficiently weak, the Soviets could use tactics which would decrease the operable area of passive deterrence—perhaps to the vanishing point. For example, we cannot afford to let an enemy believe he can safely make multiple small limited attacks on our military forces either in or outside of the United States. Cumulatively, these attacks might degrade our military system to the point where it was but a precarious Type I Deterrent, while no particular attack was sufficiently provocative to touch off a mutual-homicide reaction.

The distinction between Type I and Type II Deterrence has implications for suitable war plans. An attack keyed to Type II Deterrence objectives might well be "all-out" in the sense of using all the military resources we have. This, however, does not mean it should be uncontrolled or unlimited. All other things being equal, such an attacker should try to avoid collateral damage to civilians and their property. The attacker is not trying to punish the defender, but to influence his behavior and reduce his military and political capability. The attacker can best achieve this goal by fighting as carefully controlled a war as possible. If the attacker avoids unnecessarily provoking the defender, the defender's rationality and his fear of reprisal might induce him to fight in a similar manner. Such an attacker should simultaneously be making definite offers to terminate the war on a mutually advantageous (as compared to continuing war) basis. In a Type II Deterrence situation, these would most likely include an offer to return to the *status quo* which was disturbed by the initial provocation. Of course, in many situations a return to the *status quo* might not be sufficiently comforting to either side. At this point there may be hope for a more fundamental solution.

The relation of war plans to Type I Deterrence is far more complicated.[8] Our response might depend upon both the military and civilian damage we had sustained. It might also be influenced by intrawar negotiations or blackmail. We may wish to indicate explicitly to a potential attacker that we are capable of controlling our response and protecting our civilians from collateral effects. This might induce the attacker to be restrained himself in his first strike. This should not degrade our Type I Deterrence excessively—after all the attacker could not be sure. He would know that he would stand some risk of catastrophic Countervalue damage even though it might not be rational at the time for us to inflict it.

The notion of Controlled Reprisal sees each side engaging in a series of tit-for-tat attacks (nuclear or nonnuclear) whose objective is not the destruction of the other side's military power but the destruction of his resolve. Each side attempts by threats and actual punishment to force the other side to compromise or back down. The Controlled Counterforce, on the other hand, visualizes reciprocal attacks on each other's military power with the object of destroying the opponent's Countervalue retaliatory capability to the point where it begins to be a doubtful Type I Deterrent. The Controlled Counterforce tries to extend deterrence to the intrawar period by using the threat of reprisal or escalation to induce the other side to avoid nonmilitary bonus or collateral damage, perhaps even at the cost of handicapping military operations. If the intrawar deterrence does not break down completely, the war will end by negotiation (perhaps preceded by a period of Controlled Reprisal). The stakes in this negotiation will be the surviving people and resources; the cards will include the surviving offense, active defense, passive defense, Command and Control, and such imponderables as resolve, deception, and morale. If the intrawar deterrence does break down, then the failure of the restraints may result in much less destruction, since the controlled phase of the war may see a massive attrition or degradation of the forces available to one side or the other. If (or as) the balance of terror becomes more

[8] See Herman Kahn, *On Thermonuclear War* (Princeton, N.J.: Princeton University Press, 1960), pp. 179–87, for discussion of war plans appropriate for Type I Deterrence.

stable we can expect to see more study and discussion of the theory and practice of Controlled Reprisal and Controlled Counterforce.

3. IMPROVED WAR OUTCOME

By Improved War Outcome, we do not restrict ourselves to making the military outcome better, though this is included. We also include lessening the destruction we suffer as well as remaining able to negotiate as beneficial a settlement as possible. Because war could come even if we had the most effective Type I Deterrence, it would be dangerous to rely completely on deterrence working. Our nation, therefore, must also have the ability to fight, survive, and terminate a war. The major argument for having such an ability is identical with the usual arguments for life insurance, safety belts, and lifeboats. These things are procured because disasters can happen and not because it allows greater freedom of action. (Just because a man has life insurance he is not necessarily willing to take greater risks with his life.)

A capability to survive and terminate wars could also be of very great value, because it could bring greater freedom of action by contributing to Type II and Type III Deterrence. The objectives guiding our development of an Improved War Outcome capability will influence the kinds of systems we will procure.

The ability to survive and terminate wars requires more than the survival of adequate offensive and defensive forces during the enemy attack. Our forces must also have an effective endurance over days and perhaps weeks. Unfortunately, when one looks at many of the new weapons systems, this requirement seems to be much neglected in both design and operation. The most startling inadequacy, however, is not in the military weapons systems, but in our neglect of civil defense. To some extent, this is currently being considered, and in a few years this country may have a modest, but still valuable, civil-defense capability.

Our contemplated civil-defense capability is likely to be aimed at the Improved War Outcome objective alone. Moreover, it will not contribute significantly to "winning" a war but only to reducing the toll—possibly quite dramatically. In addition, the present program will not contribute much to either Type I or Type II Deterrence, and may indeed make both of these somewhat weaker. This is so because today's basic program would protect the population from fall-out by the use of existing structures. Most of these existing structures are vulnerable to blast and firestorm and are concentrated in cities. Aside from the fact that the safety of much of our population would depend upon an enemy's forbearance, or his inability to hit a large number of cities, a population so sheltered would make an ideal hostage for postattack blackmail or coercion. An enemy might well try to limit our response to his attack by threatening to destroy the people in such concentrated, vulnerable shelters. In other words, the enemy can try to fight a Controlled War in which the extreme vulnerability of our still unharmed population gives him an advantageous bargaining position; if we had not had the program and most of this city population had been killed by fall-out, it would then have been unavailable as a hostage. If the enemy feels he might be successful in limiting our reprisal, he will raise his estimate of the chances for a favorable outcome to any attack he launches. However, the fact that there might be more Americans left alive for an enemy to hold as hostages after an initial attack is hardly a persuasive argument against the shelter program. It is on the contrary a strong argument for improving and supplementing our present program within the limits suggested in Section 5 ("Comprehensive Arms Control") and for maintaining a strong strategic posture; one strong enough to win or successfully stalemate the military exchanges so that the enemy will not be able to achieve a superiority from which he can make extreme or one-sided threats.

Improved War Outcome also puts severe requirements on our Command and Control systems, much more severe than the requirements for a simple "go-ahead" order. We need the ability to evaluate damage, to change war plans, to improvise, to recover forces, to bargain with the enemy, and so on. Unfortunately, Command and Control systems have, in the past, basically been designed for the peacetime operation of our forces. Until recently we did not even consider adequately the capabilities that will be required to communicate the simple "go-ahead" if the enemy takes full advantage of our vulnerabilities. Much less have we considered adequately the requirements for a "war fighting" as opposed to a "war deterring" capability.

To estimate the need for any particular Improved War Outcome capability, or its probable performance, it is important to test it against many possible types of attacks that an enemy might make, ranging from an all-out attack concentrated upon people and civilian property, to a limited attack upon military forces accompanied by deliberate efforts to avoid mass destruction of civilian targets. For many reasons, the more limited types of attack in this range are more likely to occur than the city-busting attack.[9] In any event, at least today, an Improved War Outcome is both more important and easier to achieve than many think.

4. STABILITY

It is widely recognized that even if we have adequate Type I Deterrence, it is possible that a war could start in some irrational or unpremeditated fashion. For example, the war could start because of:

1. Accidental triggering of either alert force or both of them;

[9] I have discussed the different kinds of all-out thermonuclear wars at length in my book *On Thermonuclear War* and in my testimony (August 6, 1961) before the Holifield Committee. (In this context, "all-out" refers to the level of effort and not to targeting.) One of the most important distinctions depends on the target system the enemy chooses for his first strike. These can be characterized very roughly as:
1. Countervalue (attacks against people and property);
2. Countervalue + counterforce (attacks against people and property and also against retaliatory forces, i.e., bombers and missiles);
3. Straight counterforce (SAC, ICBM's, Polarises, etc., are the only objective);
4. Counterforce + "bonus" (people and property are included as secondary targets whenever they can be hit without distracting from the primary military objectives);
5. Counterforce + avoidance (people and property are carefully avoided where possible and only military objectives are aimed at).
Only (3) and (5) seem to be rational for the attacker (who would then try to use the cities as hostages either to intimidate or to try to force his opponent to negotiate), but any of these attacks could occur. Even the simplest civil-defense programs would be extremely effective in the last three cases (keeping casualties in the 1–25 million range instead of the 10–100 million). Quite elaborate programs, however, might fail to protect much more than half the population in the first two cases.

2. Misunderstanding by one side of the opponent's intentions;

3. Miscalculation of the capabilities of our Type I Deterrence;

4. Irrational or pathological actions; illogical or irresponsible gambling; and

5. Escalation or catalysis.

Almost everybody, expert or layman, worries about one or more of the above possibilities. It is therefore desirable to design our security system so that it is not prone to any of them. This can be done in two ways: by reducing the probability that incidents of the above sort can occur, and, equally or more important, by reducing the probability that such incidents could actually lead to war. After all, it is decisions, not incidents, that cause war.

The first requirement is that the system not be "trigger happy" in order to survive, that is, that it not depend for its survival on quick decisions made in ambiguous circumstances. The stability of our posture can be improved by buying well-protected systems that can "ride out" the attack and respond later, thus providing commanders with the essential time for careful evaluation and decision.

Another important way in which unpremeditated war may break out is through the "reciprocal fear of surprise attack," that is, a situation in which each side feels itself under pressure to pre-empt, mainly because it feels the other side may pre-empt. In such a situation, fear itself may make it rational and almost imperative to strike, even though the fears may be based on a mutual misunderstanding. The likelihood and danger of such a situation increases directly with the advantage to be gained by striking first, and with each side's estimate of the likelihood that the other side will strike first. The advantage to an enemy of striking us first will depend on the difference between our striking power before and after he attacks, that is, on the vulnerability of our posture. Moreover, his estimate of the likelihood of our striking him first will be increased by greater vulnerability in our posture, because such vulnerability increases our incentive to get in the first blow.[10]

---

[10] The requirement that both sides be relatively invulnerable has led some analysts to recommend that we procure only a city-busting strategic force

The likelihood of accidents and wrong decisions will also be greater to the extent that we do not have centralized Command and Control of forces, together with confidence by local command in their ability to survive attack. Decentralized decision-making about whether we are at war, who the enemy is, or even which war plan should be executed, will increase the likelihood of unauthorized actions or wrong decisions. A vulnerable centralized system can be disastrous even if it is not in fact destroyed. So long as local commanders suspect its vulnerability, they will be encouraged to act on their own if unable to communicate with the central command, even though it may turn out that the situation was due to a peacetime accident and not enemy action. The local commander who doesn't know may feel under pressure to do something before he is destroyed, not because he is insubordinate but because he is trying to do what he believes he would have been ordered to do if the Command and Control system had not failed. Thus a vulnerable Command and Control system may not only act improperly when an attack really has occurred, it may also act improperly if no attack occurs.

To summarize: if the strategic forces on both sides are well enough protected so that there is no necessity for either side to make any rushed decisions, and if the centralized Command and Control systems are reliable, it is difficult to see how a war could start inadvertently. In the absence of either of the above, inadvertent war may be a real possibility.

and deliberately weaken our military ability both to attack the enemy's strategic forces and our civilians' ability to survive his counterattack. The other side can then feel safe that we will not pre-empt. It is indeed true that if we eliminated all capabilities for Type II Deterrence and Improved War Outcome that we would have made clear our peaceful intentions. We would also have made, at least for the short run, a real contribution to slowing down the arms race. In addition, the resulting posture would be a good basis for many types of arms-control negotiations. It is also worth commenting that surrender or unilateral disarmament would also fulfill all of the above requirements. I mention this last because the pure city-busting deterrent force advocated above does amount to a dangerous kind of unilateral disarmament, dangerous both from the viewpoint of the competition between the Soviet Union and the United States and dangerous because a war can still occur, even though there have been no precautions taken for surviving that war.

I think it is well to realize that as an over-all requirement, the requirement for stability is more than just stability against accidental war or even against an attack by the enemy. We also want stability against extreme provocation, i.e., Type II Deterrence.

Herman Kahn

5. COMPREHENSIVE ARMS CONTROL

Many thoughtful and responsible students of the arms race believe that our present international order with its emphasis on unconditional national sovereignty, national egoism, nuclear deterrence, and national military forces is not going to last out the century, and perhaps not more than a decade or two. Many of those holding this belief do not deny that many successful adjustments have already been made to modern technology. They recognize the important, but often neglected fact, that the current arms race is not as uncontrolled as would be the case were narrow military, technological, and economic factors the sole determinants of military research, development, procurement, and operations. Indeed, when compared to the inherent technological possibilities, the current arms race looks more like a walk rather than a race because it is so limited by political, social, moral, economic, and doctrinal constraints on the participants. These constraints and adjustments doubtless "buy" time, but many believe that they do not buy enough time, under the given conditions, for the system to adjust itself satisfactorily by the usual processes of gradual evolution. It still seems likely that we will change the system "consciously" or, despite feasible short-run safeguards, that it will "blow up." By "blow up," I mean undergo a sudden and violent change caused by cataclysmic events with little opportunity, in advance, to influence the shape of the new world which might result.

If the system does blow up in a war or violent crisis, it is somewhat unlikely, perhaps most unlikely, that it will result in an "end of history." It is more likely to be a very serious crisis whose "solution" involves major structural changes in the international scene; it may be one of the "small" thermonuclear wars I have already discussed, followed by a viable peace; it may even be a large thermonuclear war, but one which is not an Armageddon. It is difficult to visualize—at least in the sixties—a likely sequence of events that would set back either the population or the wealth of the world by more than a generation or so. Catastrophic as this would be, it would not be an "end to history" or even an end to civilization. However great a misfortune it would be, we are not barred from noting that greater misfortunes could occur. The term comprehensive arms control should be taken not only as covering mutually desirable measures likely to decrease the probability of war, but similar measures that decrease the damage that is done if deterrence fails, both by limiting equipment and tactics; for an example of the latter one could envisage an "open city" agreement to avoid killing noncombatants away from military targets.

One approach to the over-all problem might be to try to increase the safety of the current system (Stability) while encouraging natural developments—perhaps aiding these by negotiation on *relatively* simple and apolitical technical matters such as a nuclear-test ban or control of surprise attack[11]—in the hope that the "war system" will gradually wither away to be replaced by another system, perhaps by a more or less satisfactory world government, perhaps by some other more sophisticated arrangement whose character is not now clear.

We might try to facilitate the peaceful evolution of the new system by trying to negotiate major structural changes in the international order. There seem to be few feasible suggestions.[12] I personally believe that it is almost impossible to negotiate a comprehensive arms-control agreement without a general political settlement, except as a reaction to a very dramatic event (such as a war or a crisis which resulted in the evacuation of cities). I also believe that in the absence of war or crisis, a general political settlement is itself most unlikely. I hope that the above will turn out to be a self-defeating prophecy, but it may not. One can, of course, accept the above view and still be willing to negotiate, partly because there are many political and social reasons for going through the motions of negotiating, and partly because one's judgment may be wrong. The negotiations may succeed.

There is another, possibly overwhelming reason for the study of comprehensive agreements and possibly even for their pre-

[11] Simple and apolitical as compared to agreements on important changes in the structure of the current international system.

[12] One possibility that could have far-reaching effects is a one-clause condominion on world affairs, between the United States and the Soviet Union, that they will refrain from the first military use of nuclear weapons under any circumstances and, in addition, will jointly strike any third power which uses nuclear weapons in a military operation. See *On Thermonuclear War*, pp. 240–43, for some discussion of this suggestion.

liminary negotiation. It is precisely the point of the above argument that if one does not believe in a relatively peaceful evolution, then one believes that a war or crisis will occur and that presumably we should be prepared to exploit whatever constructive things could be obtained from the event. Such a war or crisis is much more likely to result in a satisfactory comprehensive agreement if there are political and military plans and preparations to exploit the war or crisis, especially if an agreement exists ready to be initialled or if there is enough common understanding of what is needed to make it easy to arrive at agreement under pressure.

In any case the search for a less makeshift solution must go on. I would conjecture that the time available is to be measured in one or two decades rather than one or two centuries. This means to me that our old concepts of national sovereignty are either obsolete or soon will be. To many this last remark implies that we should be unwilling to risk or fight a war solely to preserve the nation-state as an independent sovereign entity. I would tend to agree. But this does not mean that we should not be willing to risk or fight a war to influence or vote on the system that replaces sovereignty and deterrence. Meanwhile we must design our strategic systems to be able to accept whatever implicit or explicit arrangements can be made peacefully—and in particular not design systems that needlessly accelerate or exacerbate the arms race. This last is not just a formal remark without content. In many influential quarters, the most pertinent question which can be asked about a new weapon system is, "How will its procurement affect the arms race?"[13]

[13] It should be clear to all that there are limits to what we are willing to do in order to protect ourselves and further our policies. I used to use the following chart in a briefing addressed to explaining this point:

Where Do *You* Draw the Line?
1. Insecticides
2. Eating meat
3. Any violence
4. Police
5. Conventional warfare
6. Kiloton weapons
7. Megaton weapons
8. Begaton weapons
9. Doomsday machines
10. Galaxy-destroying machines

This above question is sometimes allowed to dominate the issue to the point where analysts and others have refused to consider otherwise reasonable active and passive defense measures for fear of touching off an offense-defense race. (See note 10 above.) Important as unilateral restraints are, few of us are willing consciously to disarm to the point where our influence and safety depend excessively on the good will and reasonableness of the Sino-Soviet bloc.

6. TYPE III DETERRENCE

In the general category of Type III Deterrence, I place all the ways in which our strategic military capability can deter "provocative" and encourage "acceptable" behavior other than by the threat of immediate "all-out" thermonuclear war. This includes the ordinary limited war, the use of all kinds of mobilizations and demonstration tactics, the show of force, and, finally, some types of controlled war as are envisaged in a Controlled Reprisal or a low-level Controlled Counterforce attack.

Type III Deterrence is a catch-all category, covering under one heading most of the important foreign policy and military problems that actually arise. It may seem strange to use one heading for all of these, and five others to cover the nuances of thermonuclear war. I feel it is valuable to direct attention to the many interactions between the more common and immediate problems and those more directly associated with strategic warfare. This approach may seem excessively narrow to many planners, but I suspect that this is partly because most of the intellectual effort in the United States and Europe has been concentrated in the areas of Type III Deterrence and on arms control, to the almost complete neglect of the problems of the use of strategic forces. Any formulation concerned mainly with strategic forces as something which might be used deliberately or inadvertently meets with resistance not so much because it is

It is the purpose of the above chart to make it clear to both the pacifist, who generally draws the line somewhere between (3) and (5), and the more resolute militarist, who draws the line somewhere between (7) and (9), that they both believe in some degree of unilateral disarmament; that there are things neither would do, no matter what military risk results, because they will not do so.

narrow (which it is), but because of the distasteful and unfamiliar nature of the questions such possibilities raise.

Nobody would protest against a discussion of economic aid which devoted 80 to 90 per cent of its space to consideration of economic aid and 10 to 20 per cent to related and interacting problems. Similarly, a discussion of limited war could concentrate on limited war and all would understand that the distortion of narrowness thus introduced is necessary to let the author speak from his special knowledge and interests—even though policymakers would have to know of the pitfalls that this distortion might introduce. But a similarly necessary distortion to focus attention on the problems of thermonuclear war does tend to arouse hostility.

My formulation does, however, obscure some important points. Some of these obscurities can be seen by examining the following chart illustrating a sixfold division of the range of deterrence situations.

DIFFERENT DETERRENT SITUATIONS

Reprisal	Provocation		
	Strike against U.S.	Extreme	Other
Some kind of "all-out" attack	I	II	α
Other	β	γ	III

I have talked much about Deterrence Types I, II, and III. This automatically focused attention on these situations and shifted it away from what could be called Deterrence Types α, β, and γ.[14] Types β and γ Deterrence would correspond to a unilateral renunciation of the all-out use of nuclear weapons in favor of action lower on the scale of violence. As already discussed, much current military thinking is concentrated on the area of Type γ Deterrence—the use of Controlled Reprisal or Limited War to deter or correct even the most extreme provo-

[14] I am using α, β, and γ rather than A, B, and C to avoid confusion with Donald G. Brennan's Deterrence Types A, B, C, and D. See *Arms Control, Disarmament, and National Security* (New York: Braziller, 1961), pp. 25–28.

cation or attacks. This merges into Types I and II Deterrence as soon as Controlled Wars are considered. Types β and γ Deterrence also include the nonnuclear responses to a Soviet attack that are recommended by many of the peace and unilateral disarmament groups. Type α Deterrence would correspond to the usual interpretation of the Dulles massive-retaliation doctrine. This concept was probably obsolete when it was formally promulgated in early 1954 and has, in effect, been replaced by giving Type III Deterrence an expanded role.

Type III Deterrence capability is and will probably remain most important for the foreseeable future. Even if we were to achieve a strategic superiority over the Soviets so that there was a relatively one-sided balance of terror, our freedom of action would not be greatly larger than it is today. Even a relatively small strategic force may be sufficiently destructive to make deterrence into a two-way street. Moreover, even if we could not be severely damaged, we would still be obliged to use self-restraint in the use of force. At the least, excessive amounts would not be appropriate; the punishment should fit the crime. Lastly, our use of thermonuclear threats, if it is to be consistent with our other policies, must look and be both prudent and rational. We cannot go around threatening to blow up a major portion of the world or attempting to get our way by looking insane and dauntless. These strategies might be available to a totalitarian nation. They are not available to us, a democratic nation in a democratic alliance. Strategies overly dependent on resolve, on committing first, on extreme use of the rationality of irrationality, are not likely to succeed even if attempted by the West.

A more thoroughgoing discussion of the many kinds of deterrent situations would doubtless divide the row labeled "other" into many distinct categories: for example, limited nuclear strategic reprisal, limited nuclear tactical reprisal, use of conventional weapons, and then various nonmilitary responses. At this point the discussion would get unwieldy. I chose the categories I did, because I wanted to emphasize the distinction between deterrence Types I, II, and III and because some of our major problems concern these situations. If and when we arrive at a firm balance of terror with the Soviets, then the many situations included in β and γ are likely to become more important so far as policy discussions are concerned. In the still more confused situation when there are many countries with large nuclear-weapon systems, a completely different terminology may need to be devised to focus on the, as yet unknown, major issues.

CONCLUSION

Another source of irritation built into this paper is my attempt, through the deliberate use of technical terminology — jargon — to put the problems of thermonuclear war into analyzable theoretical formulations. Particularly in the area of politics, international relations, and government, Americans tend to be practical and pragmatic, almost to excess. They tend to reject attempts, real or pseudo, to build up elaborate theoretical machinery.

There are exceptions, of course. But by and large, Americans, both practical and intellectual, rarely sit down and try to draw up utopias or even far-reaching long-term programs. They tend to neglect distant problems, no matter how important; they concentrate, instead, on problems which all may agree are less important, but which are present, ready, or immediate.

This was a fine, perhaps optimal practical policy for one hundred and seventy-five years, but many now believe that when it comes to problems of foreign policy, this approach will no longer work; that, while preserving as much ability to muddle through as we can, we still need a program, blueprint, or theory of where we are and where we want to be; that we cannot meet our day-to-day problems unless we think more intensely, more profoundly, and more wisely about fundamentals than we have in the past; that the intuitive reactions of even the most experienced politicians, the most senior statesmen, the most agile pragmatists, will no longer serve, if we are to control our destiny and shape the world to come.

It is unlikely that we can do this well unless we sharpen our conceptual tools and our language. We also need better mechanisms and organizations than we have had for anticipating technical and political developments and planning to meet them. While there is always the possibility that lucky muddling through or unassisted statesmanship will get us out of the mess we are in, I find this unlikely without guidance from systematic professional work.

JOSEPH CROPSEY

•

THE MORAL BASIS OF
INTERNATIONAL ACTION

The power of nations to inflict pain, destruction, and death in warfare has been brought to such a peak that men feel themselves compelled as never before to find means for preventing that power from being used. The instruments of mutilation and devastation are tremendous and their action comprehensive to such a degree that their employment would produce effects that shock the mind, for they reach perhaps to the impairment of the human race as a whole. It is by no means easy to obtain agreement as to the essence of moral offense in general; but it is transcendently easy to obtain agreement that it would be monstrous, and if monstrous then immoral, for men to burn up the moiety of mankind and to denature the loins of those who survive.

We have not yet said what is meant by moral; but skill at definitions is not a prerequisite for concluding that every man and group of men has a duty to abstain from destroying mankind. One could go further. The enormity of exposing the world to nuclear blasts is so absolute that an absolute moral obligation is created to abjure the weapons themselves: they must not be allowed to exist, for their existence is the potentiality of the absolute evil.

It therefore appears that each nation is by duty bound to practice a voluntary restraint, to limit its own action and power of action in the interest of some good which is not its obvious, immediate self-benefit. For the sake of fulfilling a duty to the rest of mankind, each nation should to some extent deprive itself of the means to supremacy or even of defense. As we reflect on

71

this duty, we notice how well it corresponds with what appears as the notion of morality at large. Morality is a standard of conduct which guides men to recognize and show concern for others, and to act out of some larger motive than the convenience, safety and well-being of themselves.

The demand of morality may be said to be in the direction of deliberate self-incapacitation. So far as this is true, morality is in apparent conflict with policy, or in other words with calculation in the interest of the actor. This is admitted both by the friends of morality, who see it as moderating the brutal egotism of life, and by the cynics, who see it as the delusion by which the strong are seduced to abstain from benefiting from their strength. In either case, solicitude for another is put ahead of or at least alongside concern for the actor's own advantage. It is easy to imagine why the claim of morality is sometimes thought to be very tenuous.

The common violation of morality suggests that something fundamental in human nature is outraged by the demand that the interest of another be made the measure of a man's or nation's action. The demand of morality appears to conflict with natural self-love and with the power of calculation that supports it. Nevertheless, to think only of oneself is perhaps more an offense against rationality than against decency. Other men and other nations have a concrete, objective existence which cannot sensibly be ignored, not merely because they will protest and retaliate, but because, from an impartial point of view, their being and their interest are equal in importance to the actor's. If one avoids the plain folly of picking himself out of the whole human race and making a special case of himself, he will easily be led to grant that he has no right to live by one set of rules and to expect everyone else to live by another. He must keep the others in mind when he seeks to form the rules of his own behavior. He will see that the fundamental likeness of all human beings in their humanity leads to the fundamental equality of all human beings in their rights. Morality means to act with consideration for the rights of others. Necessarily we must curb ourselves in action out of respect for the objective equality of the others who exist around us. We must do so not out of any mere sentiment of sympathy, or even fear of retaliation, but out of a rational perception that mankind is a whole, while each individual is but a part and must content himself with only so much advantage as one among equals can sensibly claim.

Thus it would appear that morality as self-limitation is the dictate of reason, based upon a rational being's power of seeing his relation to others with an impartial, objective eye. Knowing his own demands and desires, he immediately knows the demands and desires of other men, for in the relevant respects the other men are exactly like himself. The intensity of his wish to live, to be free, and to set his own goals is the measure of the same wish in others. Not any moral sense, or even conscience, but bare objectivity extorts from him the concession of the equal right of every other man to the same goods that are important to him. And since his wish for the good things of life, the same wish on the part of others, and his power of understanding the equal right of those others all exist by nature, why should one not say that the moral duty of self-limitation is a natural obligation and thus binds all human beings equally?

The more we prove that the moral law is binding, the more we are obliged to explain why it is so commonly ignored in practice. Evidently, "binding" is ambiguous, meaning both "ought because it is right" and "must because it is compulsory." There is a difference between what makes justice good and what makes it obeyed. Where the two influences have little to do with each other, or even conflict, the moral system in question is defective. We must evidently look further into the sense in which a moral obligation is binding. To do this, we shall have to think further about the basis of the moral order, that basis we have been calling "objective" or rational. We are led to carry the inquiry in this direction because the standard of morality has been said to be rational and therefore binding, yet there is a gap between this rational standard and the standards of behavior actually obeyed by the rational animal.

We may begin by noticing that the moral problem is peculiar to man, in the sense that only the actions of men are subject to moral restriction. The misconduct of things and beasts is not called immorality. The reason for this is that men have a unique power to control or govern themselves. A beast can be trained, indeed, and it will show signs of apprehension when it breaks a rule, but there is no reason to suppose that it experiences anything but a fear of consequences when it does so. When it behaves well, it does so out of mere obedience. Men, however, do not merely obey; they are capable of themselves positively willing to do what is also required of them externally. They are thus unique in the whole world as willing, self-controlling, rational beings. This is a most important fact, for as a result of it, men have an overriding absolute worth or, as is often said, a dignity. The dignity of man is absolute; men therefore have an absolute moral obligation to one another, and incidentally, corresponding absolute moral claims on one another.

The word "absolute" is used in a literal sense to describe the mutual moral obligations and claims of men. The worth of man is so great that our duty to each other cannot be based upon any calculation of interest. To base our actions toward each other upon some calculation of interest leads to the contamination of every seemingly good deed: we would be truthful only to preserve our credit, kind only to preserve ourselves from retaliation, grateful only to encourage benefactions, and so on. Actions so performed would not express any recognition of man's dignity; all of them on the contrary would imply the treatment of other men as things to be manipulated, by cunning appearances, for the benefit of the actor—who would deserve to be so called for more than one reason.

It is clear that this conception of moral duty, resting upon the premise of man's capacity for willing, really rests upon the premise of man's capacity for willing freely—or, in brief, upon man's radical freedom. Now if there is a moral teaching based upon the belief in man's freedom and dignity, we are compelled to take it seriously because we regard our own political system as itself based upon man's freedom and dignity. To be true to ourselves, we might have to adopt as our own the absolute standard of morality which veers away from interest and toward uncompromising obligation, a standard that jeopardizes diplomacy or even foreign policy as we know it.

The notion of an absolute moral duty to all mankind certainly implies a solemn obligation—to our allies and to neutrals, and to our enemies no less, as human beings with an absolute worth. In brief, it seems to point toward unilateral disarmament if necessary, thus toward our voluntary extinction as a nation, as the purchase price for human lives. It seems to require of us that we remove ourselves from the path of History and submit without resistance to be overrun by the course of events, in the interest of mankind. I shall try to show that such a notion of an absolute moral obligation rests upon error and cannot be the guide to action; it does not oblige because it cannot and ought not oblige in practice.

1. The rule of absolute moral obligation is derived from a generalization about all mankind, and it pretends to oblige every man toward all of mankind. It claims a status similar to that of a law of nature. But it is a fact, as objective as any moral metaphysic, that men live not under the moral laws of nature but as members of nations under positive laws. The existence of bodies politic with different legal systems is the sovereign practical fact. The inference from this fact is that homogeneous mankind is superseded in practice by politically differentiated mankind; that laws obliging all mankind must be mediated by the legislation of the nations. The fundamental condition for the translation of absolute moral duty into political practice therefore does not exist in the world. Absolute moral duty to mankind is without a clear meaning so long as the most comprehensive active unit of the human kind is the national body politic and not the human race. When we confront other human beings, it is not simply as men but as fellow citizens, or as Frenchmen, Britons, or Russians. We recognize thus that humanity is radically divided, and the division is along lines of the divergent moral understandings and legal constitutions that inform the several political bodies. From the variety of moral foundations beneath the several political societies, two things follow: the duty of each society toward every other is affected by the character of the one toward which action is to be directed, just as our moral duty to act toward parsons and pickpockets, bearing in mind their common humanity, does not eventuate in the same conduct toward both. And second, since not all societies (and perhaps no societies) subscribe in their constituting principles to the view that there is an absolute moral duty of man to man, any nation that derived its practice from such a view would involve itself in the difficulties described next.

2. If absolute moral duty as described is to be the guide of any nation's practice, it would have to be recognized by mankind generally, that is, by all the nations or by the important nations, as the guide to their actions. If it were not, then obedience to the moral law would inevitably entail suicide, or if not suicide, then disgrace. Coincidentally, obedience to the moral law would guarantee the triumph of the immoral, of those who feel little need to obey the moral law. A moral law that brings the obedient to death and shame and guarantees the success of its violators is not fit to be discussed at length by men with practical responsibilities.

3. The absolute moral law claims to oblige us in the name of duty alone, apart from every consideration of interest or benefit, and to speak in the name of human dignity and freedom only. But we notice that to obey the absolute moral law would under present circumstances remove the last practical defense of human dignity and freedom, as will be argued. Moreover the absolute moral law is not, as it claims to be, mindful only of pure duty and oblivious of ends and consequences. It rationally regards human survival, freedom, and dignity as goods worth pursuing; its absoluteness dissolves before the higher worth of the good it aims at. If obedience to that law imperils the very goods the law is based upon and must seek to preserve, then obedience to the law is an absurdity, and the law obliges no one, although it is a very objective law.

Our first general conclusion is that moral laws are not "absolute" in their force but must be obeyed in such a way that the result of obeying them is consistent with morality or simple decency. Morality uninformed by sound judgment is theoretically, let alone practically, null. This means that we must and do believe that deceitfulness is immoral, yet espionage is not to be eschewed; homicide is baneful, yet we must be ready to destroy the enemy; intervention in foreign sovereignties is reprehensible, yet we may not hang back from it.

Historically, the belief in a rational and objective ground of morality has led to views of mutual obligation quite different from the principle of absolute duty just examined. If rational and objective mean founded on common observations that anyone can make and verify at any time, then there is no more rational and objective foundation for morality than this: that all men, like all living things, have an overpowering preference for themselves, each one devoted to his own interest more than to anything in the world, with "interest" subject to some latitude of definition but not very much. But in that case it is both impractical and theoretically unsound to argue that man's duty to man must be understood as abstracted from every consideration of interest and consequences. Human nature would rule that out. Recurring to the remark made earlier to the effect that morality is inseparable from self-restraint out of regard for others, this powerful fact of invincible self-love makes a most unpromising foundation for morality, unless in some way the law of the jungle can transform itself into a moral law.

In fact, precisely this or something like it is thought to happen; for it is clear that belligerent selfishness gives rise to conflict and mutual injury, and thus defeats itself, since it ends in destruction among the selfish parties. It was noticed long ago that the ends of self-interest are best promoted by strictly enforceable agreements to live and let live, agreements by which each binds himself to abstain from the goods and persons of the others in order himself to be immune from destruction. It goes without saying that such agreements would be not useless but dangerous to those who entered into them if there were not effective arbitrators to enforce them, and to punish violations; otherwise, faithless contractors would exploit the simple who honor their engagements.

On this view of the human situation, morality may be said to grow out of, or to be replaced by, or to be identical with rational selfishness. Selfishness dictates that each individual respect the absolute right of others, and that he and the others ratify the tenders of their mutual consideration by submitting to be ruled by laws with penalties attached. Let us call this the condition of institutionalized mutual regard.

What does this notion have to contribute to our understanding of the moral ground underlying international action, military or other? What is the character of the moral obligation that nations have toward one another? It is no other than an obligation to live by the laws that are enforced between the nations for the preservation of each and all of them, and to submit to the punishments impartially inflicted for disobedience. But what are those laws, and where are the authorities that punish the infractions? Evidently there are none of either.

If morality means to follow the dictate of survival under legal restraints in the interest of everybody's equal right to follow the same dictate, but among the nations there are no legal restraints of any significance, then plainly the nations' moral obligation dissolves into the right of naked power wielded by each country in its own behalf. Violations by one nation of another's right to survive can easily be recognized, but there is no judge to reprobate those violations and to order and execute retribution except the injured nation itself and its allies. The only mutual consideration that exists or can exist among the nations is what they extort from one another by the fear of consequences, that is, by force.

It is disturbing to reflect that if one begins with the rational and objective natural rights of men to life and security, one ends with the reduction of international morality to violence or threats of violence, and nothing more. This conclusion is unacceptable for, if admitted, it would render us incapable of judging the moral quality of Hitler's acts to strengthen the Third Reich and Churchill's acts to strengthen Great Britain. But the need and the possibility of making that discrimination are facts as rational and objective as the common impulse toward self-preservation. We therefore have not arrived at a satisfactory understanding of the moral basis of international action; where the oppugnancy of justice and interest is resolved by the reduction of the former to the latter, the moral system in question is imperfect.

In presenting the two moral extremes, the one of absolute duty to all men as men and the other of simple calculation in the interest of the agent, we have run into these difficulties: either the moral action of the one party exposes him to ruin at the hands of an immoral antagonist (with the consequence that morality leads invariably to the triumph of evil) ; or the possibility of moral discrimination disappears entirely, leaving as the only criterion of action the submoral criterion of success in survival. In either case, what begins as morality ends as immorality.

The Moral Basis of International Action

With this behind us, we can set down the requirements of a moral ground for international action, military and other. And if it turns out that no moral system can without self-contradiction meet these requirements, then we may conclude that morality is irrelevant to the conduct of nations, and all is just in hate and lust. The requirements for such a moral order are these: (1) That a nation be able to abide by the rules of right conduct without harm to itself even if every other nation in the world ignore or violate them. (2) That notwithstanding the full compatibility of the moral order with survival and victory, the rule of morality not simply dissolve into the right of the stronger, that is, the criterion of success.

Beginning again, we recur to the simplest and most generally admitted notion as to the meaning of morality: morality is self-restraint. Hitherto, we have taken self-restraint to mean a voluntary holding back either from violating an abstract precept of duty or from injuring others. The implicit supposition has been that the overriding problem to which morality addresses itself is how to define the duties or rights of men, the extreme solutions to the problem being either duty apart from calculation or calculation apart from duty. But there is no need for morality to mean either the one or the other so exclusively. This becomes clear to us when we consult the normal human understanding of what conduct deserves blame and what deserves praise. We blame people who deceive, defraud, plunder, attack, and murder; but curiously we also blame those who are vacillating, miserly, gluttonous, lewd, or craven, although it is not possible to say, for example, "gluttonous toward others." These latter defects are not primarily the sources of injury to other men. They are rather flaws of weakness, for example, the weakness of being unrestrainedly fond of some external good, or of being incapable of exercising that amount of self-control that enables a man to come to a conclusion or to suppress cruel, effete, or otherwise disgusting passions. We might note at the same time that a man overcome with the sense of duty, who plunged incontinently, that is, unrestrainedly into every situation where good needed to be done, would come under deserved censure as a dangerous meddler, especially if the only good accomplished was the salving of his conscience. There is a path between morality in the service of preservation and morality in the service of duty, abstractly considered; and that path is the one indicated by the general understanding of mankind. It follows the rule that self-restraint is not confined to the agent's acts against others but touches his character more comprehensively.

The first rule of morality is indeed self-restraint, and the first rule of self-restraint is to avoid falling under condign hatred, shame, or contempt. The corollary of this rule is that morality rests upon sober judgment of circumstances, men, and things, so that the agent will avoid the disesteem earned by folly; and that it culminates in a justified sense of self-respect. Morality, thus, is not intelligible as an abstract or formal principle but only as the sum of concrete characteristics, the possession of which enables the agent to deserve praise and respect. Morality without virtues is vanity.

What are those praiseworthy characteristics, and what does any of this have to do with the international action of the United States? The answer to the first will be tantamount to the answer to the second. Neither a nation nor a man can avoid shame if it is craven, heedless, self-indulgent, wanton in ease, irresolute in deliberation, wastrel in pleasure, squeamish in contest, faint in adversity. Virtue is etymologically related to manliness; but the relation is evidently more than etymological. What course is then open to the United States other than that dictated by the moral law undistorted by doctrinairism?

I believe that if we test this rule of morality, which rises more or less directly out of common human experience, we will find that it meets the two conditions laid down earlier as being indispensable if the moral criterion is to be applicable to the nation's action. We are at no disadvantage if all the world but us behave brutally, foolishly, aggressively, deceitfully, and in every other way immorally. Prudence and decency demand of us that we make every effort to withstand every attempt that can be made against us; to do less would be contemptible and thus immoral. To do as much would be to work toward safety through morality. It goes without saying that morality so conceived utterly excludes those avoidable deeds of massive violence that can be defended only on the premise that success justifies everything. Certainly success is not the touchstone of morality as naturally understood, and it is not sensible to infer righteousness from survival, nor vice from failure. It is indeed possible to be respectable in defeat and contemptible in victory; but it is not possible to be respectable in defeat if defeat is the result of sloth, decadence, or a failure of nerve.

By this view, war and therefore the preparation for war are, in themselves, neither morally good nor morally bad, any more than homicide is morally good or bad. The homicide of a police officer upon a fleeing criminal is morally good, the homicide of a fleeing criminal upon a police officer morally bad. War is dreadful, and the preparation for it painful; but a theory that defines the painful as the immoral is nothing but hedonism or an encouragement to hedonism, no matter what appeals it may make to sentiment, conscience, or a show of rights. War is bad but it is not bad in the way that a supine indifference to disgrace and slavery are bad, for the latter comes from moral corruption and the former only from a fearful necessity that some men cannot, because of the vice of others, avoid.

War is bad because pain and death are bad, and death worse than pain. But we must reflect on the order of things, and recognize the difference between the death of men and the death of nations. Individuals die, but those remaining make up the loss. Cities are reduced to material chaos, but in an amazingly short time the destruction is repaired. The resurrection of a regime, however, is a thing rarely seen. The Constitution subverted, liberty disappears, and the human flotsam remaining suffer the ultimate demoralization, which is not death but subjection to the unlimited will of a master. Those who would investigate war and peace as part of the moral problem may never stray out of sight of the fact that the necessary condition for all morality is freedom, and the condition for freedom is the absolute integrity of the body politic—guaranteed by the power and willingness to make war.

It is evident that morality can retain its connection with self-restraint without collapsing into self-incapacitation. On the contrary, the demands of morality, seen in their relation to freedom and honor, are more energizing than they are paralyzing. Then the question arises whether there is anything at all that could contribute to the greatness and safety of the nation for which a justification could not be found by appealing to honor. The answer to this is surely No if the appeal to honor is a specious pretext, and as surely Yes if the appeal to honor is itself honorable. But assuming for the moment that the appeal to honor is not hypocritical, what sort of act would a nation be compelled to deny itself for purely moral reasons, contrary to its urgent interest? Is there something dishonorable, for example, in espionage? In deceitful counterintelligence? In the apprehension of a rebel by means of a ruse? In the subversion of a foreign government with which we are not at war? Not one of these questions can be answered except with knowledge of concrete circumstances. The most relevant circumstance is the character of the nation doing the deed in question, and the character of the men or nation to which it is done. What should one answer to the question, Ought one to spy on his neighbors? To enter a strange house in the absence of its owner? To detain another man by force? There is no answer in the abstract, but only in the light of the character of the agent, the one to whom the deed was done, and the circumstances.

Obviously the question arises, Which nation is to be the judge of all these things? The answer is that we must judge for ourselves, both of ourselves and others, and trust that history will vindicate us when our reasons are known and our intentions are proved by the event to have been reasonable and humane. Those who raise the question, Who shall judge? do so, very often, in the belief that it is self-evidently absurd for us to be judge of our own morality. In truth it is no less, and perhaps far more absurd to hope that a reliable judgment on our morality will be brought by a poll of the nations, many of which are moved by animosity and envy, and more by ignorance. We must go forward to preparation for war, the neutralization of enemies, the adaptation of foreign regimes, and all other things needful, doing right as it is given to us to see the right, and trusting to the only judgment fully informed of our intentions, namely, our own. In another world a more schematic or precise answer could perhaps be given to this question; and if we were a petty nation in the hinterland of Africa, the question would not practically arise for us. But in this world, morality must paddle its own boat with whatever implement comes to hand;

and the problem is ours because the United States is where it is and not in central Africa. The teaching of morality may be reduced to this: we must do everything that needs to be done to insure the survival of ourselves, our friends, and our free principles, indulging neither ourselves nor others, avoiding sentimentality no less than brutality, and mindful that if we weakly hang back, we will ignominiously hang alone. Those who desire to see this wisdom reduced to a punched-tape program must await their translation to another, better universe; likewise those who wish to see it purged of all severity.

It will surely be objected that to imperil the human race on the point of honor is to inflate Quixotism from an eccentricity to a calamity. We must therefore try to keep separate in our minds these two principles of action: the one, that it is wrong and dishonorable weakly to submit to domination; and the second, quite different, that what deserves to be defended should be defended, and what deserves to be resisted should be resisted, but that it is not sober to make a virtue out of defense and resistance regardless of the worth of the things to be defended and resisted. In other words, the appeal to honor alone is defective, and must be perfected by a showing that honor is aroused in a good cause; otherwise it is suspected of being a euphemism for truculence or ferocious obstinacy. Do we have any reason for believing that the sovietization of the world is an evil commensurate with the peril created by opposing it? that it is the menace to dignity and freedom it was earlier said to be? To answer this question fully would require a full statement of the character of communism; here we can provide only the barest intimation.

Marxism begins with materialism and ends with the homogeneity of mankind. Marxist materialism differs from traditional materialism in attaching fundamental importance to the process of production, that is, to self-preservation by means of "technology," primitive or complex. The problem of preservation is primarily a technological, not a political problem for Marx. Indeed the complete solution of the problem of preservation is radically nonpolitical: when the means of production are commonly owned and production is made a wholly social process, politics, or ruling and being ruled, will cease among men. The aspiration of communism is a total solution of the economic problem by means that would reduce all mankind to a single classless, that is, homogeneous mass: a huge herd of sheep safely grazing. Human distinction is the source of the human problem, and therefore distinction must be terminated. The "heroes" will be "heroes of the shovel" and "heros of the loom": heroes of social production. This could be called the ultimate vulgarization of humanity, or the final indignity. We see it foreshadowed in the substitution of the shoe for the gavel in council, and the hairy chest for the clean collar in diplomacy. Because dignity is inseparable from distinction, the resistance to sovietization was said to be in the interest of human dignity.

What of freedom? Communism aims at life without the state, or without formal government. We are not interested for the present in the empirical question of whether the state can wither away. We observe simply that Marxism makes no provision for the form of government, for constitutional guarantees and so on, all such being impermanent and beneath its serious noncritical notice. The governments that have arisen in socialist states have therefore had to be improvised to administer the proletarian ascendancy during the revolutionary phase of world communism. They are governments singularly adapted to the stringencies of revolution—autocracies. But it may be asked, what of the postrevolutionary times, if any? No man can know the answer to this; we can only discern a presumptive answer, or a likelihood. The formlessness of the herd without distinction exposes it perpetually to the highest concentration of irresponsible authority—wielded for the noble end of administration, all other problems having vanished. More simply, a flock demands a shepherd.

The bias of Marxism toward matter and in opposition to form bears fruit in an unprecedented threat to human dignity and freedom. Honorable resistance to sovietization is thus more than merely honorable.

Readers may be pardoned for failing to see in the Soviet Union now a population of grazing sheep. Far from a fat and torpid flock, they are an active, patriotic, spirited community, exhilarated by their hard-won achievements, conscious of greatness and lusting for its gratifications. That they are all these things is a vindication, not a contradiction of what was said above: finding their revolution confronted by hindrances, they compel themselves to rise to formidable heights of exertion. They are in the irrational condition of heroically laboring to destroy the possibility of any future heroic labor, while congratulating themselves on their own heroism. It is not the self-contradiction but the menace in their doings that is our present concern, and how we must respond to it.

We are in the position of respecting and praising the sense of honor, and of discerning it well-developed in our enemy. We will prove his right to rule us if we do not prevent him from exercising it; and we can maintain our right to be free only by being in a position to exercise it. In plain language, to his irresistible force we must oppose an immovable obstacle. If we do so, we appear to increase the possibility of global depopulation, to scant our duty not to contribute to the death of mankind. Two questions then arise: Do we in fact increase the possibility of destroying mankind? Is it our duty, if the answer is Yes, to surrender to the Soviet Union in the interest of human survival?

As to the first question, the issue is in doubt, depending entirely on what happens when the engineer of an irresistible force knows himself to be opposed by an immovable obstacle. There is not one iota of preponderance on the side of the view that the activator of the great force will choose to dash it against an absolute resistance. But if he entertains any reasonable doubt that our response will be absolute and remorseless, he will have less reason to keep the peace. This means that at a certain moment we must harden ourselves to look at the beauties of peace and prepare to see in their stead a contaminated chaos peopled with human carrion. If we cannot stand this thought, we are not ready to fight and will therefore be compelled to do so—or to truckle and prostrate ourselves.

On one condition would the sacrifice of ruin not be excessive: if we triumphed and the enemy were in the end destroyed. It is absurd to say that there are no victors in war. The one who survives in freedom is the victor; the one who must humble himself and surrender his ways and institutions at the dictate of his enemy is vanquished—as much now as when men fought with clubs. Victory is as much better than defeat now as when David smote Goliath. Nuclear physics in its great productivity has changed many things, but it has not yet brought forth a palatable isotope of humiliation.

Perhaps it will be said that there can be no victory where there are no survivors. This is true enough, but inconclusive. The question is, What follows from it? The most obvious conclusion is that we must do our utmost to insure that plenty of us will survive, so that the nation can go on, in the enjoyment of victory. But it might be argued that no one could possibly survive the next war, which must come to an end with the apocalyptic death of the human race. Let us for the present accept this assumption as empirically correct. Then there must not be a next war. To argue so is plausible, but again inconclusive, for the argument tells us nothing about the form in which the cost of avoiding war must be paid. It might be that we pay for peace by abject surrender. That is unthinkable. It is unthinkable because the argument in favor of doing so is based upon the premise that, morally and politically, nothing matters —nothing, that is, except survival. The proper name for this position is not philanthropic morality but nihilism without intestines. The fortified species of nihilism also argues that nothing matters—except success. We have lost contact with the human spirit if we can no longer sense the repulsiveness of nihilism and the depravity of it in its emasculated form. If nothing matters, then human life does not matter. (Who would mourn it?) If anything matters, it is the decency of life and the possible self-respect of men. Still, where there is life there is hope for some amendment of any evil. We agree, and recommend the thought to our enemy; it deserves his consideration no less than ours. In brief, there is one cost of avoiding war which is more than we can afford: subhuman self-abasement.

Then we must pay for peace by making such a preparation for war that apprehensions for the safety of mankind will for once begin to influence the calculations of the enemy. If he is beyond or beneath a care for man's preservation, he is the manifest enemy of the race, fit to be hedged in or destroyed, certainly requiring to be diligently guarded against. If he is capable of such a care, then we need not, as truly we ought not assume the whole burden of providence, devoting our progeny as it may be to Moloch. Effectually bringing home his duty to our adversary is a far more defensible method of discharging our own moral duty to mankind than would be giving over the world to a moral enigma; for we would then be performing a sort of missionary work, animating a solicitude for human survival in places where it has been hitherto unknown or without effect.

It is a paradoxical and fearful fact that the only way we might have peace is by opening our minds to war. That way lies the presumption of safety—in war if it comes, through peace if it does not. It is not necessary to say that there is no guarantee that mankind will not be decimated and irradiated. Nature itself does not vouchsafe his survival to man: the instruments of general destruction of which we now stand in dread are inferences from principles implicit in nature, principles which have lain in darkness from eternity, waiting to be grasped and put in execution by man. We happen to be the climactic generation, in whose time the combination of man and nature seems to be achieving the critical mass. We cannot avoid our fate, but we need not be craven in confronting it. On the contrary, the ways of danger and moral decay are one. Life itself hangs by the thread of honor.

We seem to have concluded that the dictate of morality coincides with the interest of men and nations whose purposes are compatible with freedom and high-mindedness. This conclusion was the one intended.

In the course of our attempt to clarify the moral basis of international action, we have been led to take up two extreme but not unrepresentative examples of moral doctrine and a third which avoids the extremes. To simplify, the three could be said to turn, respectively, on Duty, Rights, and Honor. The conclusion has been that the first two are, for the purposes of guiding international action, imperfect, and the third is to be preferred. Supposing this for the moment to be true, of what practical value is the conclusion? Is it possible for a nation simply to adopt the moral principle of its choice for application to its international business? There is reason to doubt that this can be done with complete ease or freedom. The reason is that each nation is given its character by the elaborate set of moral judgments already embodied in its system of laws and practices. Implicit in the laws and customs is a notion of what action is just, what is proper and decent, what is worthy of esteem—in brief, of morality. As an example, we could contrast the famous system of the ancient Spartans with that of our own country now. No one would argue that we could simply "adopt" for international purposes the morality of Sparta, while our constitution as a nation rests on a radically different moral basis. If all our notions of tolerable conduct are fashioned by one system of judgments, can we act externally on another? We shall consider in the remainder of this paper the relation between the municipal morality of a nation and the demands of existence in a world of nations.

The problem is made especially severe by the kinship that exists between our general moral outlook as a community and the two moral dispensations described above as the "extremes." When we go back to the Declaration of Independence, for example, we read of man's inalienable rights—which are the same natural rights that we noticed earlier in the discussion—all derivative from the natural right of all men to self-preservation. The Declaration enumerates the inalienable rights to life, liberty, and the pursuit of happiness; the Constitution speaks of life, liberty, and property. The replacement made by the Constitution is not of the nature of a revision but a clarification: the rights to life, liberty, and property are inseparably connected with happiness, in our moral and political understanding as a nation. It is only when each man is guaranteed in his person that his property is secure, and only when he is safeguarded in his property that his person is inviolate. Our political system makes provision for translating those natural rights into a meaningful ground of civil life by wedding the institutions of capitalism to those of constitutional government. Political freedom is possible on various bases; in the Western world it exists on the foundation of certain economic institutions, and the concurrence of capitalism and modern democracy is by no means a coincidence. Liberty and prosperity, the aims of our order, are provided for at one and the same time by a principle that authorizes the individuals to act in their own behalf under the protection of a government to whose rule they give their consent so long as it defends them in their freedom to act in their own behalf. The essence of acting in one's own behalf is calculation. This is the basis for the remark made at the head of this paragraph, to the effect that deep in our own moral and political foundations there is a kinship with the extreme moral principle named after "Rights," leading to undiluted calculation.

But the assertion was also made that as a nation we have an affinity for the opposite moral extreme as well, the one called by the name of "absolute Duty." Long ago, the reduction of morality to the rules of calculation was seen to be open to various objections. One line of objection was to the effect that when morality collapses into mere calculation, patriotism or love of the common good tends to languish or to disappear. This view when broadened or exaggerated becomes the criticism that, under the reign of private calculation or institutionalized egotism, care for the absolute worth or dignity of man as man vanishes, and life deteriorates accordingly in the moral respect. Those who hold this view feel a need to oppose "human rights" to "property rights." The objection on behalf of patriotism or civic virtue found a certain expression in the yearning for republican, agrarian simplicity often voiced in our earlier history. The criticism on behalf of man as man is more characteristic of the reforming or Liberal tendency as it now is among us. What began as solicitude for a sort of virtue that can become patriotism has been replaced by a solicitude for humanity or Society, a care that need not eventuate in patriotism.

Thus our moral life as a nation vibrates between the poles of calculation and a radicalized alternative to it, the former polarizing on Property, the latter on hostility to it and on radical, undiscriminating Equality. The former is at the heart of our national conservatism, the latter epitomizes contemporary Liberalism. Neither is in its nature oriented upon the sovereign good or the good of the country as men's profound concern: neither pays heed above all to honor, the sober mean somewhere between calculation and duty.

There is indeed a lack of perfect congruity between our ruling moral predilections and the preferred moral basis of international action. But if we must act on the strength of what we are rather than what we might wish to be, there is little doubt as to the course we ought to follow. One of the two poles of our moral world stands as an encouragement to men to love their theory of homogeneous mankind more than they love their country and their countrymen, where the demands of the two come in competition. The other pole, grounded on the perhaps low but surely solid principle of calculation, is not out of contact with the intermediate moral ground of decent self-regard or honor. Husbanding our strength, gathering our allies, and preparing to avoid the supreme disaster of servility and disgrace, we at least avoid the imprudence of opposing armed brutality with impotent dogma. Our enemy is abundantly furnished with dogma, but his action is notably unobstructed by it. His moral ground contains two elements, as does our own. One of them, if made the spring of his action, would bring down his regime and his empire in instant ruin. It is no less than the replacement of political life as known on earth by an absolute morality, to be inculcated among men by the economic institutions of communism. The other is Revolution—its necessity, its goodness, its inevitability. They are respectively his end and his means. The first is never allowed to get in the way of the second, which is the ruling element of his moral nature. It behooves us to remain in touch with our adversary on this simple level in order to oppose him—undistracted by sentimental dogma which he mocks, game theory which he ignores, and all other sophistications that are wasted upon a political intelligence which rightly or wrongly regards coercion as the ultimate rationality. Under the circumstances, we may allow ourselves to be led by calculation where perhaps we cannot be taught to soar by honor.

We began by thinking of man's duty to mankind. Reflecting on morality in its connection with the deeds of nations, we could not avoid the themes of honor and nobility, or more largely of human excellence. Human excellence, as it finds its expression among the masses of men ranked in their nations, is called civilization. Whatever reminds us of civilization reminds us at the same time of our duty to civilization, which means in practice to civilized men. What begins as a reflection on duty to man ends, under the influence of a glimpse at human superiority, as a reflection on duty to civilized man and to civilized nations. The way to discharge our duty to civilization is to sustain it where it exists before trying to inspire it where it never has been. Upon this point, remote from doctrinairism, the morality of calculation and the morality of honor come within sight of one another. The resulting gain in strategic competence brings them within earshot of one another. We must not despair if they never join hands.

David R. Inglis

•

TRANSITION TO DISARMAMENT

The question as I see it is not whether the arms race should be allowed to continue unchecked. I assume we are all agreed that the completely unlimited upward arms spiral is too nearly certain to end in the final catastrophic explosion, for it has no other terminal facilities. The question is rather whether one can introduce some restraint with sufficient symmetry between the contending nations as not to invite dangerous adventure, and, if so, what forms of restraint should be promoted.

A good case for unilateral restraints in weapons placement and doctrine, preferably reciprocated, has been made by Robert Osgood; but he considers it only as a holding operation for the next decade or two. Beyond that, he sees the need for some new nonmilitary mechanisms for regulating international relations, but depends on the hope that these will arise as a by-product of unilateral acts which avoid the regulating mechanisms of formal agreements. In this he seems to me to depend somewhat less on a miracle of sudden universal good will without prior practice than does Edward Teller, who has repeatedly postulated world government as the end result of making all present decisions on the basis of additional military strength as the sole criterion.

Herman Kahn, too, recognizes that the effectiveness of deterrence is only temporary and that some form of world government must be the end result. He goes further and expects disarmament. However, he so despairs of human political capability that he expects it to achieve a disarmed world only after being shocked into action by the terrible catharsis of nuclear war.

Walter Millis, while recognizing military confrontation as a temporary necessity, aptly discusses the irrelevance of superior nuclear capability for the current world competition in the "revolution of rising expectations." He concludes that military and defense policies should be directed toward realization of a demilitarized world.

All of these analyses, so different in their views of contemporary political and military needs, converge on disarmament as an ultimate necessity, although they do not agree on when and how it may be approached. There are many people who would write off the prospect of a substantial progress of disarmament in the next few years as wishful thinking in this political world. During the period 1952–60, I was among them and considered instead a controlled nuclear test-ban agreement as the form of initial restraint most likely to be attainable.[1] The reasons for despairing of disarmament after 1952 were, first, that the need for inspection during stages of disarmament seemed incompatible with the existence of military secrecy during those stages before disarmament is virtually complete; and, second, that the then-new H-bomb technique greatly amplified the military significance of small amounts of secreted fissionable material.

The first objection has been removed by the availability of the new region-by-region disarmament technique, the revolutionary significance of which will be explained later. The second difficulty looms less ominous now that we have with some luck become accustomed to living with the H-bomb for almost a decade and see greater importance in questions of the speed and reliability of weapons delivery than in the simple existence of H-bombs.

At the present stage of world political and military development, the attainment of a drastic degree of disarmament soon, down to a low level of equalized nuclear armament to serve as a transitional deterrent, seems by far the most practicable and the most desirable primary goal. (Whether enough people will appreciate its practicability to make the goal attainable is another question.) The low-level transitional deterrent stage is intended to give time for the development of more permanent world institutions permitting essentially complete national disarmament

---

[1] D. R. Inglis, *Testing and Taming of Nuclear Weapons*, Public Affairs Pamphlet No. 303 (1960). Also articles in the *Bulletin of the Atomic Scientists* (1954-60).

as the ultimate goal, with greatly reduced danger of accidental war in the meantime. Such a low-level transitional deterrent can be safely attained only by formal agreement and systematic control. Limited arms-control measures, such as the test ban or the proposal of roughly reciprocated unilateral elimination of primarily first-strike capabilities, should be considered as desirable secondary goals if they do not interfere with the pursuit of the primary goal, or as last-ditch stopgap measures if the primary goal proves unattainable after diligent pursuit.

Proponents of minimal arms control without formal agreement tend to discount the likelihood of reaching a formal agreement, partly because of the failure of what might be called half-hearted attempts to reach agreement in the past. For instance, Mr. Osgood writes: ". . . the depth and intensity of [the] political and ideological conflict, and the distrust which it breeds, severely limit the utility of formal agreements as instruments of military restraint and co-operation. . . . The area of military restraint and co-operation must be enlarged and stabilized chiefly by reciprocal unilateral arms controls and by informal and tacit understandings."[2] There are indications that similar confidence in informal, unilateral measures rather than formal agreements is also held by influential members of the present Administration. If so held, such a view can partake of the nature of a self-fulfilling prophesy, for it tends to preclude diligent search for formal agreement.

ARMS LIMITATION AND A TEST BAN

The various degrees of arms limitation to be considered and compared fall into the categories of test bans, arms control, and disarmament, the latter two terms being not mutually exclusive. Of these, a permanent test ban and any substantial form of disarmament require formal agreement, whereas the minimal forms of limitation sometimes known as arms control may not.

For almost three years negotiations took place in the relatively calm atmosphere created by a moratorium on nuclear testing by the great nuclear powers (not including France). During this time military pressure built up for at least another round of testing, presumably on both sides, and largely for the immediate

[2] "The Uses of Military Power in the Cold War," p. 6.

purpose of trying out those improvements which have been developed since the last tests. Though the end of the moratorium may seem to darken the atmosphere of negotiation, it might in a sense act as a release valve to reduce this military pressure and improve the chance of reaching an agreement. By dramatizing the need for stopping tests, a new round of testing should intensify the influences favoring a test ban and of course does not change the rationale.

The arguments are still strong for trying to make a nuclear test-ban agreement with the Soviet Union along the lines which have been discussed in the protracted negotiations. Even if such a nuclear test-ban agreement should stand alone, not followed by other types of agreement, its arms-development-limitation feature would be valuable in preventing the development of more unstable situations. If it were followed by an agreement banning and controlling missile testing (except as part of a joint peaceful space-exploration project), the limitation on arms development would be still more effective. These test-ban agreements can be considered quite separately from disarmament. They have value in themselves, and need not necessarily lead to disarmament.

One of several valuable features of a test ban is that it would help preserve the technical possibility of disarmament, in case we should later decide that disarmament would be a wise course. Its immediate advantage is that, by preventing refinement and proliferation of nuclear weapons, it would help prevent the likelihood of war from increasing rapidly. But that same refinement and proliferation, if allowed to go unchecked, would make it more difficult to introduce effective disarmament controls, if at a later date we should want a disarmament agreement. By putting on the brakes with a test ban, we would help keep disarmament within the realm of possibility.

The main drawback, the reason for caution in considering a test ban, is the possibility of evasion of the control system. Particularly during the early stage of a nuclear test-ban agreement, with sufficient trouble testing under awkard conditions, a few relatively small bombs, about a thousandth as big as big H-bombs might be tested in secret in a closed country like the USSR (although they probably would not be tested, with the incentive so small). The likely consequences of such evasion, if it should happen, have been grossly exaggerated in statements which have received prominent press coverage. When the consequences of such severely limited testing are viewed in a reasonable perspective and compared with what the great nuclear powers have already learned from years of uninhibited testing and development, the advantages of a test ban seem very distinctly to outweigh this disadvantage, quite apart from any thought about disarmament.

Being a timid step toward arms limitation, a test ban has a relatively limited value and its price is small in terms of deviation from traditional expansionist military policy. While one may argue that our failure to attain it at so small a price shows the impracticability of seeking more drastic agreement, one may equally well point to the incentives in so mincing a step as insufficient. Particularly in 1959 when the USSR seemed interested in obtaining a test ban, the price was exaggerated on the side of the United States in terms of the possible military consequences of a few small-scale clandestine tests evading the control network. In 1961, when the United States had attained a more balanced view of these matters and was ready to negotiate, the USSR had apparently ceased to feel the incentive sufficient. It now seems likely that their changed attitude was caused by a military demand for renewed testing following the deflation of their confidence in missile-site secrecy by the excellence of the reconnaissance photos revealed in the U-2 incident, although the change might instead have resulted from their judging it too late to persuade the Chinese to join a test ban. The price of a controlled test-ban agreement always seemed exaggerated to the USSR because of a distorted view of the extent to which test-ban controls need to interfere with military secrecy. The Soviets place great value on their legitimate advantage of superior military secrecy, and it seems likely that the far greater incentive offered by drastic disarmament may be required to persuade them to relinquish it.

The "Troika" demand of a three-man administration of test-ban controls, which came several months before the Soviet resumption of tests, seemed to be a Soviet way of saying they did not want a test ban, and in retrospect seems to have signalled their decision to prepare for test resumption. Contrary to common belief, however, it is not at all clear that a test ban could not be designed to work with a three-man administration, for the all-important selection of sample seismic events for on-site inspection (after the certification of their technical characteristics by the administration) is to rest with the proposed twelve-man council (not with the one-man or three-man administration) on the basis that "the other side chooses." In any event, the pendulum of Soviet policy swings, and efforts should be continued to obtain a test-ban agreement.

If both sides go on testing there will be a tendency to reach a common level of nuclear technology, for there is a limited amount to learn. Thus we cannot hope by further testing to regain the long lead we had before the Soviet test resumption. A test-ban agreement, or indeed any arms-control arrangement, will probably be achievable only if based on a recognition of approximate equality by both sides. A controlled test ban would still have great value to us in promoting stability, and we should now have a better chance to negotiate it than earlier when we were trying to freeze a very distinct superiority in nuclear technology. The more thorough preparation of positions, made possible by expanded study facilities within our government, should help, though the newly established Arms Control and Disarmament Agency seems to be getting off to a slow start and needs increased support if it is to meet the need.

MINIMAL ARMS CONTROL

The terms "disarmament" and "arms control" refer to a wide variety of possibilities, for most of which the two terms may be used interchangeably. Disarmament as we shall here discuss it involves control (although unilateral disarmament does not) and most arms-control proposals involve some reduction of arms levels. The name "arms control" has become popular lately among planners seeking some strategy of moderation as an alternative to the completely uncontrolled arms race. In some contexts it refers to a sort of self-control with little or no disarmament, and may even call for an increase in some categories of arms.

In the competitive haste to transfer from manned bombers to missiles as the main instrument of mutual deterrence, we are reaching an interim stage which is even more explosive than the longer-term situation need be, so far as the present two great nuclear powers are concerned. Many of the missiles are being installed and quickly-constructed open pads, extremely vulnerable to an aggressive strike. They form no part of a threat to retaliate, because, being exposed, they would be destroyed by the enemy's first blow; that is, they have no "second-strike capability." They are thus extremely provocative. They seem to tell the adversary that they are intended only for a first strike and sorely tempt him to strike first in anticipation.

Our motivation in setting up the Atlas missiles so quickly and cheaply is, of course, not the intention to strike first; but it may look that way. It is really probably a mixture, which no one quite understands, of public relations (the intention to impress ourselves and our allies with our apparent prowess) and a desire to add to the first-strike requirement of the adversary—he would have to be ready to expend some missiles to knock out these and much of our Strategic Air Command before using his surplus on cities. But we have placed our launching pads wrong on both counts. We have succumbed to convenience and the myopic pressures of local chambers of commerce and have placed many of the launching sites near cities like Laramie and Denver. We have further found it convenient to cluster the launching pads in such a way that one attacking missile could knock out several of them. Thus they do not increase the adversary's requirement as much as they should.

Suggestions for minimal arms control start with a little self-control and propose that we should first eliminate these mistakes, concentrate on hard or mobile missile bases with second-strike capability, and urge the USSR to do likewise. The reasoning is that it is in the interest of each of us to convince the other that we have only installations with second-strike capability, and enough of them to provide an effective deterrent to a first strike. Provocation would thus no longer be built into the weapons system. It still might be exercised as an instrument of political policy.

The advantage of such a minimal approach is that it would not be very dependent on the effectiveness of an inspection system, if at all. If each side is anxious to convince the other that it has no "soft" bases, for example, a mutual inspection might be agreed upon in the form of a joint observation-satellite program capable of observing the absence of open launching pads but not capable of observing underground hard sites or of giving up-to-the-minute information on rail-mobile systems.

One trouble with this approach is that it provides no apparent end to insatiable military appetites for more of the most advanced weapons when the number available to potential enemies is not reliably known. Advocates of such an approach seem to think that reasonable restraint would be exercised, in spite of the fact that the military value of the restraint required is enormous compared to what would have been demanded in 1959 to make possible eager negotiations for a test ban on the part of the United States. Then we choked on the relatively small matter of what might be learned under difficult subterranean conditions from a few tests a thousand times as small as those already carried out by both sides under ideal conditions of observation. It is hard to foresee how to engender confidence that the other side is reciprocating moderation in numbers of weapons, unless we have the kind of inspection that is available only through formal agreement and at the price of more than minimal arms restraint. One proposal is that both sides should decide to have only weapons so expensive that they cannot afford them in astronomical numbers; specifically, that they depend only on Polaris-type submarines for deterrence. Here again there seems to be no assurance of compliance and no way to force a matching policy on the Nth nations for whom the cheapness of other types of nuclear missiles would be attractive.

Another part of a minimal arms-control system might be an agreement, tacit or otherwise, not to make civil-defense preparations. Once it is agreed that both sides have massive striking power, and yet power incapable of forestalling a counterattack, the civil populations of countries, and particularly the urban populations, automatically become the hostages preventing the intentional outbreak of war. The arms race can be extended into the new dimension of trying to reduce the vulnerability of the hostages, but if it is done on one side, it will be done on the other. The effort will largely cancel itself out, particularly because it will probably merely escalate military requirements for numbers of missiles to wipe out populations.

David R. Inglis

Thus a tacit agreement to avoid the inconvenience of serious civil defense might constitute a reasonable part of minimal arms control. Even now, societies are sufficiently open that there is here no real difficulty about verification.

A controlled test ban combined with some form of minimal arms control would represent an improvement over the frightfully hazardous course we will otherwise follow. It would make war less likely, but it would still be far from safe. The numbers of weapons would go on increasing at least until the most demanding estimate could find no need for more. With very large numbers of missiles on instant alert on both sides, and in an increasing number of countries, accidental war, sooner or later, through technical or human failure, would still be much too likely. There is strong incentive for eagerly seeking more drastic arms-control measures in search of more substantial improvement of the situation.

INSPECTION VERSUS SECRECY IN HALFWAY MEASURES

To go further with arms control, one is faced with the problems of verification of compliance with the provisions of an agreement in a distrustful world. In the atmosphere of distrust that is inevitable when we have the dubious stability of a posture of opposing military threats promoting conflicting national interests, the relinquishing of military capabilities in a trade between the two sides is a serious step. Although the balance is dangerously accident-prone, as a rational deterrent it is a rather rugged balance in the sense that it would not be upset by a considerable disparity in the destructive capabilities of the two sides. This is largely because the prospective destruction of hostages is so much more grim than is necessary to constitute an ample deterrent against rational attack. Thus considerable latitude might be acceptable in the attempt to keep disarmament concessions carefully balanced in military value on the two sides. A reasonable and potentially acceptable disarmament plan must, however, achieve at least a very rough balance of concessions.

We cannot hope to devise an orderly procedure providing instantaneous complete disarmament and simultaneous assurance of compliance. Either partial or complete disarmament seems more acceptable if it can be achieved by gradual stages, with a reasonable degree of inspection and assurance that each stage has been completed before the next is undertaken. Several plans have been written defining the stages in terms of the percentage of each category of weapon or installation to be given up at each stage. At least one such plan[3] went into detail trying to balance the military values of the concessions by the two sides at each stage, in spite of the asymmetries in prowess in different categories, by requiring different percentage reductions in a given arms category by the two sides at each stage.

Such staged plans run into the difficulty that military secrecy is incompatible with unhampered and effective inspection. One cannot inspect for hidden missiles to ascertain what percentage are being retired, without having a chance to discover the exact location of missile launching sites. Complete disarmament, if it were politically acceptable, would have one unique technical advantage. With complete disarmament, neither side would have military secrets to guard, and thus would have no military reason for not letting inspectors roam at will. Even Premier Khrushchev, who seemed so allergic to inspectors when partial disarmament was discussed, has emphasized that the USSR could afford to admit inspectors freely to verify compliance with a plan for complete disarmament. This is a very simple and logical deduction, and we should consider it fortunate that the Soviet leaders recognize it. However, standing alone, it is not very useful, until we can find a way to get from here to there without taking too much of a risk along the way.

THE RANDOMIZED REGION-BY-REGION DISARMAMENT PLAN WITH PRIOR INVENTORY

Recently there has been suggested a way to circumvent the difficulty that inspection and military secrets do not mix, a way to take advantage of the Soviet leaders' view that inspectors should be acceptable when (and thus presumably where) there are no military secrets. The plan, as proposed by Professor Louis Sohn of Harvard, is so simple as to make one incredulous at first

[3] Inglis, Flanders, Friedman, and Jaffey, "A Specific Proposal for Balanced Disarmament and Atomic Control (1952)," *The Centennial Review* (October 1962).

that it could have any unique significance. On appreciating its revolutionary efficacy, one wonders why it was not invented long ago. That it was not is a sorry indication of the inadequacy of official studies. If there had been established a National Arms Control and Disarmament Agency on an imaginative scale in 1951, when it was first publicly proposed,[4] rather than with a small start in 1961, this simple idea might have been available to bring American disarmament policy into fruitful focus during the formative years of Soviet policy following Stalin's death. The present Soviet avowed interest in total and complete disarmament (in four years!) may indicate that it is not yet too late to work out a reasonable compromise, passing in a very few years to a low-level transitional deterrent, with complete national disarmament under an international force as the real ultimate goal.

The proposal contains three special features. First, instead of disarming gradually by categories of weapons, it is proposed to disarm gradually by regions within each country. Since inspectors and geographic military secrets do not mix, the proposal seeks to eliminate the secrets, such as missile sites, and introduce the inspectors simultaneously in one region as it is disarmed. This eliminates only a fraction of the national military power at one stage and is thus an acceptably gradual approach to disarmament. The regions are chosen to be of equal military value and it is not known in advance which is to be disarmed until each stage commences. Second, there is a preliminary inventory of all military installations in all the various regions, without disclosure of their exact locations. Third, at the time a region is selected to be disarmed, a detailed inventory must be submitted agreeing with the preliminary one and disclosing locations of equipment within that region. This provides an opportunity, by thorough inspection of the region, to verify the original inventory on a sampling basis and to establish confidence.

To explain a bit more fully, the region-by-region plan starts out by having each nation divide itself into, let us say, six regions, which it considers to be of equal military value. (If it divides them unequally, it may be left short in the late stages.)

[4] D. R. Inglis and D. A. Flanders, *Bulletin of the Atomic Scientists,* VII, No. 10 (October 1951).

A complete inventory of arms and military installations within each region, but without their exact location, is submitted to an international control authority. Inspectors may be spread thinly on the borders between the various regions in advance. Then, on a given day, the first-stage regions to be disarmed are chosen in an unpredictable way, either by lot or by choice of the other side, and the international inspectors are quickly concentrated on the borders and airports of that region to seal off arms transport. Detailed inventories, with locations given, are then submitted for these chosen regions and the inspectors disarm them. The important point is that the inspectors then have a year or so to search the region very thoroughly with complete access, to verify that there are no hidden arms. This constitutes a random sampling of the previously submitted inventory, and on a sampling basis verifies that it is fairly dependable. Thus some confidence is developed, each side has less distrust of the other, and, as the successive steps proceed, region by region, the sampling becomes more adequate and confidence is further increased. Thus disarmament and inspection spread together gradually over each country, region by region. When the time comes to disarm the last region, each side has strong reason to believe that the inventory submitted by the other is accurate, and ideally each should be able to trust the completeness of the sudden disarmament of the last region in its turn. Two important features are, first, that a nation would not know which region was to be the last, and so could not prepare it in advance differently from the others; and, second, that there must be some sort of inspection of production facilities (which will not disclose geographic military secrets like missile sites) to prevent production of important weapons in the last region while the next-to-last is being disarmed.

The plan makes effective use of the situation that only with thorough disarmament and with the abolition of geographic military secrets may inspectors be given free access, a situation which is just as reasonable for a region as for a whole country. There are, of course, numerous details which need to be worked out, and skeptics can doubtless make gaming studies of cheating and countercheating procedures. But as a general approach, this "randomized region-by-region plan with prior

David R. Inglis

inventory," as proposed by Professor Sohn, seems so superior to earlier proposals as to open new doors to practical consideration of serious disarmament. It holds promise of providing a reasonable escape from the long-term dangers of the infinite arms race.

SPECIAL PROBLEMS OF THE LAST STAGE

One advantage of the randomized region-by-region plan is that it is adaptable to a variety of disarmament procedures and objectives. It might, for example, aim to eliminate long-range missiles and aircraft, but leave defensive radar networks, mobile ground-to-air missile units, heavy tanks, and artillery. Or it might lead to complete disarmament down to the level of machine guns for police purposes. We may assume that each side will be cautious lest the other side get some substantial advantage to upset the balance of deterrence at some stage of the disarmament process. There should be no difficulty about going to essentially complete disarmament in each of the various regions until the last, because the arms in the remaining regions would still be nearly enough balanced.

This region-by-region technique is an important innovation in the disarmament field because it circumvents what appeared to be a technical impasse. Some may belittle it as a gimmick, and claim that it is a change of national attitudes and not a mere gimmick that is needed to make disarmament possible. If this be a gimmick, it is a crucial one, for it greatly reduces the need for changed national attitudes. Without it, great trust is needed at some point, perhaps trust that the other side will not try to evade the conditions of disarmament in spite of the inadequacy of minimal inspection designed not to interfere with military secrecy. With it, nations very suspicious of one another's intent to evade where evasion is possible can still reasonably enter into an agreement in which growth of confidence is based on thorough inspection to verify faithful performance. If two or more very suspicious nations recognize the great mutual benefit of genuine disarmament, this plan makes the difference between technical possibility and impossibility of exploiting the mutual interest.

Transition to Disarmament

The region-by-region plan is, however, only a means to pass safely from one level of armament to another. Ideally, it could take us right down to complete and universal disarmament if we were to be ready for it by the time the last region would be disarmed, say, in six years. It is to be assumed that we will not be ready. It will probably take much longer than that to resolve the ground rules of the competition between East and West in the "revolution of rising expectations" to a sufficient degree that trust can be generated in a decision-and-command apparatus for an international police force. For this reason, the region-by-region plan should be used to reduce the level of strategic deterrence to the lowest and least accident-prone level that can be agreed upon to maintain an interim military balance, or transitional deterrent.

The purpose of establishing a transitional deterrent stage is thus to make it possible to get started on a very substantial degree of disarmament now, without waiting to solve all the other problems of the troubled world first. The important fact here is that the conduct of limited power politics in local situations, where both sides intend to stop short of triggering a general war, is independent of the exact size of the strategic deterrent. The strategic nuclear forces which both sides are planning to build up in the next few years are to be far in excess of what will be needed to inflict unacceptable damage and to promote restraint where national interests conflict.

The answer to the question, How much damage is unacceptable? depends on how mad we get in making our assessments (or, perhaps, how sober, in Herman Kahn's language!). The case has been made that an attack of about 1,500 delivered megatons on the United States (or, specifically, 1,446 megatons as discussed in a 1959 Congressional hearing), that is, something of the order of 300 five-megaton H-bombs, would be acceptable in the sense that a recognizable nation would survive and recuperate to prepare to fight or otherwise pursue its national interests again. This is thought to be the order of magnitude of initial attack that might be experienced in about this year, 1962. However, it is only about one-tenth of the order of magnitude of the estimated stockpiles of H-bombs of each of the great nuclear powers. One can reasonably talk of an initial attack of "only" a few hundred bombs because of temporary problems of delivery during the transition from the manned bomber to ICBM's. The normal course of the transition will lead to the construction of thousands of deliverable bombs. It must perhaps be considered within the realm of possibility that they will be opposed by other thousands of antimissile missiles carrying H-bombs of comparable magnitude, but if so, this will merely step up attack requirements to assure that something of the order of a thousand or more get through. Judged in relation to their purpose, that is, to act as an effective deterrent by being able to inflict unacceptable damage, such enormous attack capabilities will "overkill" by a large factor.

A transitional deterrent could be very much smaller than this and still be effective. It could be designed to maximize the unacceptability of its damage and to minimize its likelihood of initiating accidental war. It would be sufficiently invulnerable that several enemy missiles would be required to knock out one missile, so an enemy limited to approximately an equal force could not afford to use part of his supply in a counterforce strike. The whole force would be regarded as aimed at cities, to exact hostages as efficiently as possible. They would surely not be opposed by antimissile missiles, so could be counted on to get through even if such defense weapons should prove to be technically possible. Under these circumstances, a force of the order of 50 missiles on each side should suffice as a threat of unacceptable damage. It would be capable of eliminating all large cities and killing of the order of one-fourth of a large population by direct blast and fire. In the context of deterring rash aggressiveness where national interests conflict, this is unacceptable damage.

There are doubtless several ways in which such a force could be arranged so as to be inspected and yet retain sufficient uncertainty of location as to be invulnerable. One way is to have the 50 missiles deployed in an unknown way among 200 hard sites, or "silos," of which some hide real missiles and some are empty or hold decoys. They could be subject to occasional inspection on a regional basis, and subject to secret reshuffling among the silos within each region in such a way that the inspectors would know the exact deployment of only a few of them at any one time, and yet after covering all regions would know the exact number of missiles.

NATIONAL DECISIONS AND THE DISARMAMENT GOAL

There are several important decisions which have to be made on questions of national policy closely related to the problem of making a transition to disarmament. It is vital that these decisions should be made with a view of their effects on achieving the disarmament goal, and not in a short-sighted way, solely in relation to temporary military expediency.

One of these is our policy on civil defense. We have seen that it is closely related to the problem of arms control, and that a lack of serious civil-defense measures on both sides may be an important aspect of a system of transitional deterrence which is relatively accident-proof because of its simplicity. Conversely, civil-defense preparations on one side will beget them on the other, and both will step up attack requirements. When, after a period of readjustment, the attack requirements will have been met, the expected damage will be as great as before, and nothing will have been gained except increased complexity, increased danger of accident, and increased military demands on the competing economic systems.

The Administration's interest in some initial steps of civil defense is based on the hope that it will provide us with a slight advantage during the period of readjustment, to save lives before stepped-up attack requirements have been met. It has little or no logical relation to the Berlin crisis, which was apparently used as an event creating an atmosphere in which the public would accept at least a first installment of civil defense. This was the wrong reason and the wrong time to get really serious about civil defense. The decision so to do should wait until all reasonable avenues of negotiating arms control have been exhausted, or until the adversary takes a serious civil-defense initiative which forces us to follow suit.

Another pending decision concerns technological unemployment, which calls for serious economic adjustments closely related to the problems of arms limitation. With the growth of machinery to replace the muscle of man and the consequent enormous gains in productivity, it is truly remarkable that the increased variety of goods and services provided by technological innovation has come as close as it has to providing full employment. I am not an economist, but it seems to me wishful thinking to believe that consumer demand within one advanced nation or group of nations can long overcome the problem of technological unemployment. An ever-increasing supply of leisure time is a natural part of our technical advance. With a fixed relation between working hours and compensation, this creates serious problems of distribution. It is most important that we recognize that we have been postponing the difficulty by means of arms expenditures. This is a stopgap measure. The problem must be faced and solved on a long-term basis.

Because there is a strong tendency to vote according to one's "stomach," that is, according to one's fancied economic interests, important decisions in a democracy must be economically acceptable. As long as we are greatly dependent on the arms-expenditures stopgap, a national decision in favor of serious arms limitation will be very difficult.

More far-reaching cures of technological unemployment are apt to be very slow to develop. The availability of a substitute stopgap would be helpful. Feeding the world's hungry mouths has been suggested, and is surely a worthy undertaking. Its drawback as a stopgap is that it requires skills and facilities very different from those required by modern weapons systems.

In the third area of national policy, a bold beginning of space exploration has already become a major element of the competition in prestige between East and West. For purposes of prestige, it is claimed that the motivation of the race is largely for the advancement of science. The ease with which funds are made available is probably to be attributed also to the expectation that there will be military applications of the technology developed. Indeed, the program was initiated by the military development of missiles, and it is impossible to distinguish clearly between the scientific and military motivations. It is clear, however, that large and expensive parts of the project are motivated primarily by scientific ambition. There is apparently no limit to how large these parts of the project might become, and still retain some scientific justification, if unlimited facilities were available.

In the judgment of most scientists, I believe, there is much less scientific justification of these space undertakings, per dollar expended, than there is in other fields of science. If we are looking for ways to advance fundamental science, there are other ways in which the money could be better expended. There is no compelling scientific need to put a man on the moon in this decade or on Venus in this century. On the other hand, there is definitely *some* scientific justification. The decision whether and when to do these things might thus reasonably be made on the basis of other considerations.

In planning the economic transition to disarmament, it is very desirable to have some substitute use for a substantial fraction of the skills and facilities now being used for military missile production and development. For this purpose, large-scale space exploration is ideally suited. It could, to some extent at least, serve as a substitute stopgap measure while our economy is being adjusted to accommodate technological unemployment. Larger expenditures on science and other aspects of culture should, indeed, become a permanent feature of the adjustment.

From this point of view, it is quite wrong to enter on a large-scale space program concurrently with unlimited military missile production. Space exploration should be held in abeyance pending a substantial arms-limitation agreement, thus making the seeking of that agreement politically more feasible. To carry on the two programs simultaneously means building up the skills and facilities to a higher level than would be required for the military program alone, thus making them a more serious drug on the market in case of disarmament. Programs that were sequential rather than concurrent would keep the level more nearly constant.

The space program now being initiated may be considered quite large, but could presumably be made much larger. It would seem desirable, for the reasons given, to postpone this enlargement, but prestige considerations will preclude this unless an agreement can be made soon to do so in both East and West as a peculiar sort of pre-disarmament accord. If a greatly enlarged space-exploration effort cannot be postponed, this very fact emphasizes that the best time to get started on disarmament is now, early in the build-up, before various aspects of the problem, including this economic aspect, become worse. At a later time, there will remain the possibility of stepping up the space program still further as a partial economic compensation for eliminating military missile production. In any case, as far as possible, the pace of space exploration should be moderated to encourage and complement the transition to disarmament.

Aside from these somewhat technical matters of civil defense and technological unemployment, there are other broad aspects of global strategy that should be coupled with the quest for disarmament, if arms limitation is to be made a major goal of foreign policy. There are a number of important places, such as Berlin, where the immediate aim of Western policy is to stand firm, in order to deny success to an Eastern policy of nibbling away at the borders. One reasonable objective of this Western policy, in the short run, is to foster Eastern desire for disarmament and for removing from the military realm entirely the competition of East and West. (As a long-term policy, simply standing firm forever is too dangerous, as it requires repeated risk of nuclear war by repeated exercises in brinksmanship.) The practice of standing firm, even if for the short term, involves making moral pronouncements of a seemingly permanent validity (e.g., "our sacred obligation to the people of West Berlin").

It is important that, in the process of standing firm by means of military threats, we should not lose sight of the need for a long-term policy to supersede this short-term posture, nor of the need to consider some questions negotiable, for the sake of achieving long-term ends which are not negotiable in the short-term context. In particular, the setting up of nuclear-free zones in Central Europe and in the Asia-Pacific sphere should be considered negotiable, for the sake of achieving disarmament, even though this may seem unattractive in the short term because, for example, it could mean the loss of a fancied prospect of German unification, which seems to be the price of retaining valued divisions in NATO.

Above all, in all these judgments, we must not lose sight of the overriding fact that our present course of unlimited competition in the build-up of armaments is not leading us to a satisfactory situation, that to risk nuclear war in several crises per decade among a growing number of nations is to guarantee eventual disaster, and that each important decision bearing on the possibility of disarmament should be made in such a way as to favor the transition to disarmament.

NOTE ADDED ON GOING TO PRESS

This essay, first written in mid-1961, starts off with the assumption that we desire to check the unlimited upward spiral of the arms race if possible. Since 1961, however, this desire seems to have had no influence in the planning of the congressional appropriation for missile production. We are now scheduled to have at least 1,600 missiles in 1964. The production rate is thereby so drastically stepped up that we will very soon be producing about four times as many missiles *per year* as we now have altogether, in spite of our recognition that in 1962 we have at least three times as much missile striking power as does the USSR.

In this situation it would seem—for both sides—more important to achieve disarmament agreement very soon than to wrangle over what percentage of the missiles is to be retired in the first stage: whether 10 per cent in the first year, as we have proposed at Geneva, or 50 per cent, which would come closer to the Soviet position that most, but not necessarily all, nuclear missiles must be retired in the first stage. It is regrettable and frustrating that the USSR has too long refused to recognize the efficacy of the region-by-region disarmament plan or of the related region-by-region inspection plan suggested in the United States disarmament proposal of April 18, 1962. However, this delay in the disarmament negotiations is no reason for us to abandon also the logic of arms control.

Establishing a missile preponderance so overwhelming as to make plausible a counterforce attack, even though it is accompanied by the expressed hope of sparing cities in that attack, is quite the opposite of arms control as discussed in these essays. The newly stepped-up production rate seems to mean that, in its deeds if not in its words, the Kennedy administration has now, unfortunately, succumbed to the short-range view and has practically turned its back on both arms control and disarmament.

Mulford Q. Sibley

•

UNILATERAL DISARMAMENT

In this paper we shall maintain that (1) military power in the modern world cannot in the long run defend anything valuable nor can it be used constructively for the attainment of political and social goals which most articulate Americans seem to profess; (2) if the contentions of the first point be sustained, it is stupid to maintain a military establishment: instead, the United States should disarm whether or not other powers do so, and its disarmament should proceed through a series of planned phases and within a rather drastically altered context of public policy; (3) such a policy might well result in competitive disarmament, but in any event would provide a more effective way of defending the American people against possible aggression than reliance on armed might; and (4) although typical objections to unilateralism may possess a measure of validity, full recognition of this will not basically impair the case for unilateralism.

I

At the outset, we might ask ourselves what the naïve child in Hans Christian Andersen's tale *The Emperor's New Clothes* might think of contemporary military policy; for Scripture tells us that God often grants wisdom to babes and sucklings and denies it to the old and experienced. The child would in its innocence wonder how grown men could expect to advance morality through threats of mass annihilation; how disarmament could be brought about by building up armaments; how security could be promoted through accentuation of fear; and how democracy could be upheld through development of "over-kill."

One can conceive the child shouting out: "But all this doesn't make sense. How can morality be advanced by threats to kill? How can building large quantities of missiles prepare the way for disarmament? How can inculcation of fear lead to security? How can democratic government be protected by stating that under certain circumstances we are prepared to reduce a hundred million living human beings to lifeless things?"

In the fairy tale, the child's cry "But the Emperor has nothing on!" immediately broke the hypnotic spell which up to then had dominated the actions of court and people alike. It then became obvious that the Emperor was unclothed. With respect to the questions we are imagining the child to ask, however, it is not so simple; for the spell which has Americans in its grip is far more powerful than that which deluded Emperor, court, and people. Put directly and starkly as the child has stated them, the questions about military policy would appear to be rhetorical. But so much like *Nineteen Eighty-Four* is 1962 that many Americans would find the child's queries highly novel—as if one were to doubt that the Ministry of Peace *was* concerned with peace or the Ministry of Truth with the discouragement of falsehood. We have become so involved in the ostensible sophistication of gamesmanship and the rationalizations of our intellectuals that we neither ask the child's questions nor seem to be perturbed when a few naïve adults actually support the child.

This paper aligns itself with the child and asserts what appears to be a major proposition implied in the innocent's questions: that a policy resting on the threat deliberately to kill millions of human beings is *prima facie* immoral, regardless of the agency issuing the threat or the ends avowed by the agency. But the paper also avers that the policy is unwise from the viewpoint of the ends it avows. We may say that it is immoral and therefore unwise and useless.

But in what ways is it unwise and lacking in utility? Here there is much to be said for Walter Millis' excellent analysis of military power. Without necessarily subscribing to all the statements in his article, we can certainly agree with him that military power in the middle of the twentieth century—and whatever may or may not have been true in the past—has hardly any ability to defend a modern state, to provide a foundation for ultimate disarmament, or to assist in the development of solutions for basic social and political problems.

It has little ability to defend a state because the more a national state piles up its weapons the greater is the tendency for its competitor to do the same, thus accentuating an arms race which, if unchecked, will lead to nuclear war. Although it may be argued that American military power kept the Soviet Union from moving into Western Europe, this is increasingly being doubted. Mr. Millis rightly questions the proposition, as did Ambassador Kennan. Even if it be held, however, that possession of military power by this country was a factor in preventing Soviet expansion westward during the fifties, it can surely be urged that the contemporary development of competitive armaments in Europe is doing little if anything to promote political stability. In fact, it would seem obvious that nuclear power competition is enhancing instability; and the mutual fears which give rise to competitive armaments are grossly magnified by the possession and build-up of the armaments themselves. In particular, the rearmament of West Germany is the source of increasing uncertainty and fear on the part of the Soviet Union and Eastern Europe as a whole. The "protection" which national armaments afford is at best a very temporary one; and the European situation illustrates how even this tends to be more than counteracted by the long-term insecurities and probable war for which their existence is in part responsible.

In Asia, it can hardly be said that possession of great armaments by the West has been an important factor in checking Chinese or Soviet aggression. That aggression is basically economic and political in nature and only economic and political measures can be expected to stem it—if, indeed, it can be halted at all. To the degree that the United States concentrates on military defense in Asia, it is, therefore, ignoring the major problem and making it even more difficult to defend legitimate American interests.

As the arms race quickens its pace and we pile missile on missile, we not only promote war-making political instability in Central Europe and fail to halt aggression in Asia, but we also make it increasingly difficult psychologically to think in other than military terms. True, we have developed the Alliance for

Progress with Latin America and inaugurated the Peace Corps —both of which have potentialities as alternative means of defense. Fundamentally, however, we still place our major confidence in military might and with every new commitment to it we find it harder to carry out nonmilitary defense. Thus we increase our expenditures on economic assistance but at the same time add billions to the military budget. Our whole attitude is fixedly military, and other methods are looked upon, at best, as ancillary or peripheral.

The situation might not be so perilous if it could be assumed that the arms race might go on indefinitely without increasing the risk of nuclear war substantially. But any assumption of this kind is surely naïve. Even if one maintain that military measures during the past fifteen years have "deterred" nuclear war in some measure—a proposition which is doubtful at best—the probability of a failure of deterrence in this sense is enormous. As Sir Charles P. Snow argued in his address before the American Association for Advancement of Science in 1960, every year that the arms race continues brings us closer to a nuclear conflict. Such factors as the very real possibility of accidental war and the enhancement of irrationality through fear immediately come to mind.

And once we are engaged in a thermonuclear war, the possibility of "defending" the United States is reduced to a minimum. What is the meaning of "defense" if we lose forty to eighty million people? And in what sense can the nation-state be said to "survive" after such a slaughter of human beings with its accompanying social disorganization and almost inevitable development of autocracy? It is utterly dishonest to claim that "national defense" is possible under such circumstances, whether one define it as preservation of human lives, perpetuation of a given political order, or protection of either material or spiritual values. The British Ministry of Defense frankly admitted as much in its 1957 White Paper on the subject: the great cities, it said, could not be protected and citizens should recognize that fact; "defense" would be confined to the air and missile bases from which attacks on enemy cities would be launched. As Sir Stephen King-Hall has put it, the Ministry in effect told the British people that, although they could not expect the government to defend them, they could take comfort in the knowledge that while they were dying the government would be destroying millions of the enemy. One wishes that our Department of Defense would be as honest; for although there are important differences between potentialities for military defense of the United States as compared with Britain, the development of military technology tends increasingly to reduce those differentials.

Thus, while for the sake of argument we can grant certain temporary successes of military "deterrence," its general and long-run effects are to lead us to ignore valuable methods of nonmilitary defense and to bring us closer to the nuclear war in which meaningful defense is impossible.

Even short of nuclear war, the very commitment to mammoth military defense is changing the character of American life to such a degree that the old values we are presumably defending tend to fall by the wayside. Erich Fromm has pointed out, for example, that the continuing arms race "creates certain psychological effects in most human beings—fright, hostility, callousness, a hardening of the heart, and a resulting indifference to all the values we cherish."[1] The arms race, moreover, because it requires both intensive and extensive technological development, accentuates the tendency of modern Western culture to transform the means (technique) into the end of life itself. Thus man becomes even more of a robot. In the United States, the virtual idolization of military defense has helped to wipe out any organized opposition to military conscription; yet the traditional "American way of life" had as one of its basic tenets the notion that military service should be voluntary. In devoting a very large proportion of our intellectual resources to planning for destruction we prostitute the gifts with which we are endowed. And the "military-industrial complex," against which former President Eisenhower warned us, continues to grow in influence and power. Finally, if the civil-defense planners have their way, we shall be subjected to even greater military-like regimentation in the name of the "defense" of the "American way of life."

[1] "The Case for Unilateral Disarmament," in Donald G. Brennan (ed.), *Arms Control, Disarmament, and National Security* (New York: Braziller, 1961), p. 190.

It is sometimes said, of course, that we need to build up American military defenses in order to win the struggle for disarmament. The most popular version of this proposition— and one heard with great frequency during the past fifteen years —asserts that if only we can build up enough military power, we can "negotiate from a position of strength." This presumably means that we will have greater bargaining power at the conference table. But there is little if any evidence to support this doctrine. A hard empirical examination would seem to show that possession of military might and the attitudes which accompany it tend to increase our delusions. We take refuge in the illusion that missiles provide protection and find it even more difficult than before to give them up: the very build-up which we claimed would enable us to negotiate imposes its own imperatives on us. We tend to reject apparently reasonable proposals automatically; and we can always rationalize our rejections on the ground that the new scheme for disarmament would allot to the other side a few more missiles. Since we continue to believe that missiles can defend, the possession of a few extra ones by the "enemy" is looked upon as dangerous.

A recent version of the "military power for disarmament" thesis holds that we should build up particular kinds of weapons systems—those, that is, which would provide "second-strike" capabilities but could not be interpreted as indicating any "first-strike" intentions. In some way, the other side would reciprocate (either formally or informally), and thus each side would be in a position where it could not be crippled by a first blow but could always effectively retaliate. Once this situation of stability had been attained, the argument goes on, the way would be paved for gradual multilateral disarmament or even independently adopted unilateral acts. Stability would reduce fear and negotiations could proceed under the presumed protection of second-strike potentialities by both sides. From the very beginning, moreover, each party would be willing to reduce or eliminate those types of arms which are useful primarily for first-strike purposes.

There can be no denying the attractiveness of mutual stabilized deterrence proposals for those who still believe that arms can defend. With their combination of decreases in certain types of weapons and increases in others, they appear to be very sophisticated indeed. They seem to maintain military defense while simultaneously providing for a "realistic" approach to disarmament.

Yet there is a kind of speciousness about them. Their very complexity leads one to wonder whether they could ever be adopted with any consistency by one power, let alone two or three. Although we should not belittle possibilities of informal understanding, schemes for mutual stabilized deterrence imply so much understanding and reciprocity that one wonders why multilateral disarmament agreements could not be attained directly and without all the involvement of "arms control." But the most serious weakness of such proposals is that they say little if anything about continued weapons research. Without stabilization in research, any stable deterrence achieved would be highly temporary and immediately subject to disruption by new discoveries. Perhaps one of the most significant phenomena in the whole arms race is the rapidly increasing magnitude of sums devoted to devising more effective weapons of mass slaughter. This will probably continue until men change their fundamental attitudes to military power. Only when they decide that military defense cannot defend will they be willing to give up technological research into military defense.

Finally, not only can military power not defend, not only will its development fail to provide a path for disarmament, but it cannot serve constructively to help in a solution of mankind's major modern problems. Mr. Millis' paper rightly points out that it can do nothing to assist in the "revolution of rising expectations" within the underdeveloped segments of the human race. In fact, any great emphasis on it detracts greatly from this objective: men cannot eat guided missiles, or develop agriculture by means of bombers, or protect themselves from the monsoons with thermonuclear weapons. Military power will not help us in planning for resource utilization nor can it teach us how to limit the size of families. Any contribution it can make to technical efficiency and social skills is purely incidental.

It cannot assist us to expand institutions of international co-operation. These depend for their vitality on human intellect, will, emotion, and eagerness to experiment with new forms of collective life. The development of a genuine international police will owe far more to the science of civil administration and the experience of such great systems as that of the London metropolitan police than it will to the military.

It should be obvious, too, that reliance on military power will not serve to propagate any more than it can defend democratic institutions. Here again, social invention, experimentalism, imagination, and gentler forms of social pressure are the keys. Military power can only add to the problems which confront us in planning for democratic development.

In view of considerations such as these and of others which are so admirably set forth in Mr. Millis' essay, the unilateralist asks himself why any nation should deliberately keep a military establishment. If the military cannot defend in any recognizable sense and if it cannot serve positively to help in a solution of the world's major political problems and dilemmas, then how can anyone support its utility? But if it is not useful—and, is, in fact, dangerous—then the only rational approach to military power is unilateralism. At this point, however, Mr. Millis seems to hold back. He takes us up to the conclusion but then says he is not recommending that the "United States should immediately and unilaterally divest itself of its nuclear arsenals and other military defenses."[2] He admits that a "good theoretical case" can be made for unilateralism and goes on to maintain that "it would in fact redound more to the real security and welfare of the American people than any other course." But he thinks that "the time has not come when it would be humanly possible to translate theory into practice."

It is precisely here that the present paper parts company with the Millis position. In general, that is to say, it accepts the Millis analysis of military power but, unlike Mr. Millis, it attempts to spell out what appears to be the logical conclusion in unilateralism. We cannot say with any certainty that the time has not come to advocate the policy which Mr. Millis admits is an inference from his analysis. The very working out of a detailed unilateralist policy, together with excellent critical treatments like that of Walter Millis, may be the means for making the policy more acceptable. Mr. Millis' examination of

2 "The Uselessness of Military Power," p. 41.

119

military power since the eighteenth century is itself one of the most persuasive arguments for unilateralism; and if the author himself can be persuaded through his study of the problem that a unilateral divestment of military power would "redound more to the real security and welfare of the American people than any other course," why cannot others be convinced also? To hold that they cannot be won over would appear to imply that they are not open to rational persuasion.

The fact is that men do respond to careful analysis and to rational appeals; and although there can never be any assurance that enough will be convinced to effect a change in policy, this possibility should not be foreclosed. Persuasion, however, depends not only on demonstration that present policies are not working but also on the details of an alternative policy. To these we now turn.

2

Once we are convinced that military power is "useless," we are immediately driven to formulate not merely an alternative military policy but also radically different social, economic, and international proposals. For military and nonmilitary policies are so interdependent that if one is changed drastically, the others will necessarily be affected. Thus unilateralism as here conceived is much more than a military policy: in fact, it touches on issues which at first seem very remote indeed from problems of military power.

Unilateralism is both negative and positive. It rests upon an utter disillusion with military power as a method of defense and sees it as a prelude to disaster in the modern world. At the same time, it maintains that there are far more effective modes of defense than the military.

What would be the shape of a unilateralist policy?

We should have to begin by assuming that a substantial body of opinion had come round to the view that military power was useless. This state would be attained as men came to see the world realistically and as education and propaganda became more effective. Citizens would question the rationality of expending greater and greater sums on military defense, when to all appearances reliance on the military could at best deter only in a strictly limited sense while in the long run preparing for wholesale destruction. Finally, a Congress and President committed to an exploration of the unilateralist position would be elected and would decide—after consulting religious, moral, political, labor, business, and professional leaders —how to work out the details.

The over-all objective of such a policy would be to prevent war and to assist in the establishment of machinery for peaceful change. Hopefully, it would do this in a number of ways. First, it might evoke reciprocal responses from the remainder of the world. Second, even if the response were not immediately forthcoming, it would stop the arms race; for while other states might continue their military establishments, it is difficult to imagine their continuing to increase their expenditures on arms. Third, a consistent policy of unilateralism would make it possible for the United States to devote its energies to the discovery and development of an effective defense scheme. Once central reliance on the military had been renounced, there would be a real incentive for the working out of nonmilitary methods. Fourth, it would be designed to strengthen international organization; for a nation no longer using obsolete military methods would necessarily have to think of international organization as a vital substitute. Finally, it would contribute to the establishment of an international atmosphere within which alleviation of tensions could more likely take place. It would not itself eliminate all sources of conflict; but it could assist in making them far less dangerous for the survival and welfare of the human race.

There are various ways in which policy-makers might work out the details of unilateralism. Here it is assumed that even after a government favorable to the policy had been chosen, there would be many pockets of opinion that would continue hostile. Since the changes envisioned would be so drastic, both these antagonistic sectors and the favorable majority would require some time to understand the implications of the general policy. Technical problems, too—those, for example, involved in a destruction of weapons and in conversion from military to nonmilitary production—cannot be solved overnight. Planning, moreover, always involves many contingent factors: it must assuredly allow for the unexpected and make provision for a certain flexibility in implementation. These and other similar considerations would seem to call for a somewhat gradualist approach. At the same time, however, the process should not be unduly protracted lest its dynamic effect on the politics of the world be weakened. An overly extended period, in addition, might tend to lengthen the time during which (in the minds of some) older methods of defense had lost their effectiveness (such as it is) and newer means had not yet been developed: this would, so many might argue, create a kind of disadvantageous "twilight" period committed neither to military defense in its present sense nor to the nonmilitary devices envisioned by the new scheme.

In casting up the balances as between a rapid and a long transition, we might suggest that six years would be about right. During this time, the new policy-makers would lead the United States from its present state of reliance on "over-kill" to that of a unilaterally disarmed nation having correspondingly altered social and economic policies.

The plan would divide the six years into three phases or periods. The first might well be designated as that of public preparation and education and would continue six months. The second, extending for possibly 18 months, might be called that of nuclear disarmament. During the third, covering the remaining time span, the central concern would be "conventional" disarmament. Each of the three phases would, of course, involve not only military policy in the narrow sense but also radically changed international and socio-economic commitments.

In spelling out the details of the three periods, we are not proposing a rigid blueprint but are rather attempting to illustrate the kinds of policies which might be envisioned. Actual experience from month to month might well alter the details and some aspects originally seen as falling into the earlier developments might be postponed to later dates.

FIRST PHASE

The first six months would be characterized by an intensive effort to inform both the American people and the world of the philosophy underlying the new policy. Political leaders would seek to dramatize as well as inform. Through presidential press conferences, Messages to Congress, diplomatic representations, public statements, and periodical articles written by spokesmen for the administration, the general basis for the new attitude would be laid down. Writings such as Mr. Millis' essay on "The Uselessness of Military Power" would be reprinted in millions of copies, translated into 68 languages, and distributed all over the world. Leading spokesmen for the new policy would offer to debate those still clinging to military defense. Television and radio would be filled with the discussion, which in one sense would be simply a continuation of the presidential campaign that had resulted in the election of the new government.

Meanwhile, on the diplomatic front, the Secretary of State would announce that as part of the new outlook, the United States was offering to extend diplomatic recognition to the Chinese People's Republic. The Secretary realized, he would state, that the Republic would not necessarily accept recognition in view of the Formosan problem; but he would be happy to negotiate on all the issues involved.

One month after the announcement on China, the President would state that he had just appointed a committee to study plans for conversion from a war-preparing to a peace-building economy. The committee would work out detailed proposals for constructive uses of resources now devoted to armaments and would report early in the Second Phase.

In whatever disarmament commission or conference was then in session, the United States would accept the latest Soviet proposals as a basis for negotiation, proclaiming in the process that since it was in any event committed to a process of unilateralism on principle, details of inspection had become far less important than before. While it hoped eventually to gain a formal international agreement on armaments, the United States Ambassador would announce, this country would in any event go beyond the requirements of the agreement: the latter would be very important in stating the public law of the world, but the United States was no longer concerned to possess as many or more missiles than any other nation. No doubt the Soviet would look upon the statement of our Ambassador with skepticism and see it as a propaganda smoke screen; he would probably withdraw the Soviet offer, announcing that the Soviet looked for deeds and not words.

To provide the deeds, the Secretary of Defense would proclaim that this country was withdrawing gradually from its military bases abroad. Within a year they would all be abandoned. The Secretary would point out that even in a military sense they had been obsolete for some time; while from the viewpoint of international policy they had undoubtedly contributed to world tensions. He would also announce a policy of gradual military disengagement in Central Europe and invite all powers concerned to discuss its detailed basis. As for the United States, he would conclude, it would be militarily disengaged everywhere within six years.

The Secretary of State and Secretary of Defense would issue a joint statement making public the President's decision to abandon testing of thermonuclear weapons. This would be explained as a preliminary to Second Phase disarmament.

Meanwhile, at the White House, the President would summon reporters to hear news about a new defense agency. It would be called the Non-Violent Resistance Administration (NVRA) and would be charged with the task of preparing plans for nonviolent resistance to any military occupation of the United States. A preliminary scheme, as a matter of fact, was already drafted and Congress was being asked to provide the necessary legislation and appropriations. Very shortly, the President would add, volunteers would be called for; and an Advisory Council of those familiar with techniques of nonviolent resistance—labor leaders, former freedom riders, students of the Gandhi movement, and pacifist theoreticians—was being established. Among the techniques to be used would be the strike, civil disobedience, and social ostracism. Toward the end of the six-month period, the President would announce cessation of the manufacture of all nuclear weapons.

By the end of the First Phase, the world would certainly not be what it was at the beginning. No doubt the major reaction on the part of Iron Curtain countries would be one of public skepticism but private uncertainty. Whether multilateral negotiations for disarmament would be helped or hindered is difficult to predict. On the one hand, it might be argued that they would be facilitated, since the United States would now not fear the possibility that, under some multilateral arrangement, the Soviet Union might emerge with more missiles than the Americans possessed: in the end, the United States proposed to get rid of all its missiles whatever the Soviet Union might do. On the other hand, the radical nature of the new American position would be so startling that the Soviet might initially become more suspicious about any agreement; it would not be able to believe that any nation could alter its policies so drastically and hence might suspect some secret design behind the American statements and even behind such acts as withdrawal of military bases. Moreover, the first reaction might include the judgment that the Soviet would gain enormous advantages as a result of American disarmament. Why, therefore, should it sign an agreement for the reduction of its own arms?

In the long run, however, we are suggesting that American policies would lead to reciprocal disarmament which might then be formalized in international agreements.

One thing would seem certain: by the end of the First Phase, no nation-state could afford to ignore the plans outlined and already partly implemented. Whether skeptical, angry, or favorable, foreign ministries and public opinion generally would have to develop responses to the American plans and actions. The United States would no longer be simply reacting to "aggressions" and intitiatives from abroad but would itself have seized the initiative in its effort to break through the arms race and to set forth alternatives to military defense.

SECOND PHASE

In the Second Phase, the central theme would be unilateral divestment by the United States of its capacity to wage nuclear war. Like the First Phase, it would be characterized by a series of dramatic announcements and actions spaced in such a way as to keep the opinion of the world on constant alert and to challenge others to emulate its actions. The steps might conceivably be arranged in somewhat the following order (although again flexibility should be emphasized) :

The President would announce that the numbers of nonviolent resistance trainees had been increased to more than

100,000 and that by the end of the phase it was expected they would total 200,000. As disarmament proceeded, he would state, many would be trained at West Point, Annapolis, and Colorado Springs service academies, so that by the end of the Third Phase the academies would have been completely taken over by the nonviolent resistance program. Of course, many other locations for training would also be required.

Two months after this announcement, the President would decree the abolition of espionage and counterespionage services under provisions of an act already passed by Congress. Many employees of the former agencies would find employment in the Non-Violent Resistance Administration and others would be absorbed by the vastly expanded government information services which would now be engaged in the serious task of explaining the rapidly developing unilateralism.

A little later the central announcement of the phase would be made in a presidential message to Congress and simultaneously in releases by the Secretaries of State and Defense. Acting under a previous authorization by Congress, the President would state that

1. All nuclear weapons were being destroyed and all establishments devoted to their manufacture were being diverted to other uses.

2. The chemical and bacteriological warfare branch was being abolished.

3. Physical facilities of the chemical and bacteriological warfare branch were being turned over to the World Health Organization, which had expressed its appreciation and its eagerness to use the facilities for its own experiments.

4. Foreign governments and the United Nations were being invited to send inspectors to check up freely on the process of nuclear and chemical-bacteriological disarmament. Later they would be invited to inspect conventional disarmament as well.

One month later, the Committee on Utilization of Resources, which it will be remembered had been appointed during the First Phase, would report. It would announce the principles to be recommended for employment of resources and would point out some of the difficulties. In general,

1. It would argue for public expenditures rather than tax reduction, on the ground that the public sector needed to be greatly expanded both domestically and internationally. Calling attention to such factors as economic underdevelopment both abroad and in the United States, it would announce a program to begin as soon as approved by Congress.

2. American contributions to economic development abroad would gradually increase until by the end of the six-year disarmament period they would total about $25,000,000,000 annually, to be administered by a United Nations agency under rules which would insure that the resources would be utilized as efficiently as possible for productive purposes. Training of skilled personnel would have a high-order priority. The $25,000,000,000 annual contribution would continue until the United Nations and the nations involved certified it to be no longer necessary.

3. The Committee would go on to state the other purposes for which resources formerly devoted to military ends would be used. Again, the principle of gradually increasing sums would be carried out. By the end of the Third Phase, the following annual sums would be employed indefinitely for the ends noted:

a. $2,000,000,000 in the training program for nonviolent resistance.

b. $1,000,000,000 to purchase birth-control equipment for those who wish to use it around the world, the scheme to be administered by the World Health Organization.

c. $2,000,000,000 to help support new world universities in Europe (on the site of former American military bases), Africa, Asia, and Latin America, the universities to be administered under machinery to be set up by the United Nations.

d. $500,000,000 as the American contribution to a world police system.

e. $1,500,000,000 to an internationally administered fund for scholarships and fellowships.

f. $18,000,000,000 for such domestic purposes as slum clearance, expanded education, and retraining and support of workers no longer employed in the war economy or likely to be displaced by socially approved technological changes.

The Senate would approve elimination of the Connally (self-judging) reservation to United States adherence to the International Court of Justice, and the President would announce United States willingness to accept international police on its soil for the direct implementation of what he hoped would be a rapidly developing world law. The President would also propose to the United Nations the establishment of regional courts (together with the appropriate world codes) for the settlement of cases and controversies between and among citizens of two or more nations.

The Secretary of State, on behalf of the government, would ask the United Nations to assume administrative control of the Panama Canal. He would state that since the Canal was an international waterway, administration by a single nation was inappropriate. Simultaneously, he would call upon other nations to surrender their nationally administered international waterways to the United Nations. The United States had concluded, the Secretary would go on, that the best way to strengthen international organization was to confront it with concrete tasks of administration. Discussion of abstract principles was excellent, of course, but the more the United Nations became involved in such practical tasks as control of international waterways, the greater would its authority and power become. In the end, he would maintain, the development of world order depends on either voluntary surrender of prerogatives or compulsory renunciation; and the former was by far the best method.

The Second Phase might well conclude with a general report to the world on the progress of unilateralism. It would indicate the number of foreign inspectors residing in the United States; some of the problems involved in disposing of nuclear weapons; progress in retraining those displaced through nuclear disarmament; state of the nonviolent resistance scheme; difficulties involved in expansion of economic development; and frustrations experienced in the administration of unilateralism.

The main lines of policy would now have been laid down and nuclear disarmament achieved. The chief tasks of the third period would be to provide for orderly conventional disarmament, plan carefully for the full implementation of economic development, round out the program for other expenditures, and strengthen the nonviolent resistance scheme.

Conventional disarmament would proceed through reduction of every category of men and material at the rate of approximately 25 per cent each year until at the end of the four-year period armaments and organized military force will have ceased to exist. If deemed desirable, a few thousand men could be kept for purposes of national police work, although it should be emphasized that the operations of a true police system are quite different from those of a military force. If former soldiers were recruited to the police, they would need thorough retraining. If international policemen were stationed on American soil, the national and international police would, of course, co-operate in matters of mutual concern.

Conventional disarmament would naturally result in initial unemployment not only among those who have served in the armed forces but also within the ranks of industry. As in the other phases of the disarmament effort, no one displaced by the elimination of arms would lose his income. During the transition from his old employment to his new he would be supported at public expense and, if necessary, retrained for an alternate occupation.

It would be particularly important to keep a watch on the scheme for economic development. As resources for this purpose increased with the decline in military expenditures, the temptation for wasteful and inefficient use might grow. High-level, international co-operation would be required, too, to make sure that the resources were employed for publicly beneficial economic development rather than to assist the elites in the several underdeveloped countries to expand their own conspicuous consumption. It should not be forgotten, of course, that disarmament would itself help in eliminating elites having little popular support; for unilateralism would clearly imply a refusal to sell the arms without which many autocratic regimes would collapse.

As expenditures grew in volume with progress in disarmament, consciousness about their purposes and implementation would no doubt increase. Some of the expenditures could be terminated after relatively brief periods of experimentation: for example, once free birth-control materials had been available for a number of years, it might be feasible and desirable to have local agencies assume the costs. The American program would evoke reciprocal responses by other nations. In the long run, as a matter of fact, the objective should be to promote co-operation in public expenditures, so that interdependence rather than dependence would be the rule. But the assumption would be that American initiatives could constitute possibly the most important stimuli for joint efforts.

Finally, the phase would witness a strengthening of the nonviolent resistance scheme. By the end of the six-year period possibly a half million to a million individuals will have been trained in the techniques of nonviolent action and the population as a whole educated in the meaning of nonviolent resistance. No nation in history will ever have prepared so thoroughly and systematically to offer nonviolent resistance to any invader; and the very scope of the plans would afford much room for imagination and adventure as well as challenges that could involve death. In the event of invasion, resistance leaders might be arrested and shot; but others would have been carefully trained to take their places. Transport, communication, and other systems could be paralyzed through planned non-co-operation if an invader should try to administer them; and even school children could and would be taught how to undercut any effort to impose an unwanted system.

But we should not think of nonviolent resistance as the only ingredient in the new defense system. All measures adopted to implement a policy of unilateralism would, in fact, constitute significant parts of nonmilitary protection. Disarmament would be a concrete recognition of the uselessness of military power. Utilization of resources formerly devoted to military ends for economic development and other peace-building purposes would tend to alleviate tensions and to promote eventual equality of conditions and opportunities, thus checking in some measure any temptation to use military violence. Surrender of many prerogatives to international organizations would strengthen agencies of world order and administration and promote international co-operation. Policies of this kind, then, in conjunction with the planned system for nonviolent resistance, would constitute the new "defense" scheme. And the argument of this paper is that such a scheme would be far more likely than military power both to prevent the utter destruction involved in modern war and to defend the physical lives and legitimate cultural interests of Americans and of all "civilization."

3

In assessing possible results of unilateral disarmament, it is hardly necessary to dwell on the difficulties of prediction in matters of this kind. There is no historical precedent for the policy proposed, any more than there is a real precedent for the kind of military and technological situation in which we find ourselves. But it can be pointed out that the most successful effort in the direction of disarmament came as a result of unilateral initiatives: for three years, there was a ban on the testing of nuclear weapons which came about through the unilateral initiative of the Soviet Union and a reciprocal response by the United States. Moreover, we should never forget that the arms race itself has been the result of unilateral initiatives and competitive responses.

A unilateralist policy, while its formulators might hope for reciprocal action of some kind on the part of other nations, would not assume the inevitability of favorable responses. But even if other states continued with their feverish military preparations, the unilateralist statesman would continue his program; for given his premise that military power is useless, he would see no reason to resume stupid policies simply because others continued them.

But would other states in fact continue to build armaments in the face of American unilateralism? There is good reason to doubt it. The voluntary renunciation of military weapons and of secrecy by the world's greatest military power could not fail to alter the international situation drastically. Moral initiative would pass to the United States and other nations would be compelled to react consciously in some way to the radical change in the international atmosphere. Because the alteration in policy would be so fundamental, we cannot assume that the attitudes they espoused before unilateralism would necessarily remain the same. To the extent that those attitudes were animated by fear, for example, they would necessarily be reshaped; for few can deny that unilateral disarmament would remove one basis for fear, at least on the part of the so-called Eastern bloc.

Let us turn to the Soviet Union as an example. Within it, there are many internal pressures for reduction of armaments. Economic development is a high-order priority for Soviet statesmen and manpower needs in this sphere are enormous. Part of the motivation for partial reduction in conventional arms during the fifties lay in the desire to augment manpower for agricultural development. If the United States removed its military bases and carried out a full-fledged unilateralist program, there would be a very strong movement within the Soviet Communist Party to reciprocate in some degree. Although great skepticism about American purposes might well prevail at the beginning of the program, its concrete implementation according to plan would probably produce a favorable response on the part of many Soviet statesmen.

It may be claimed, of course, that the Soviet would simply use its great military power to "take over" the West and the United States. But this is to assume that the Soviet has such intentions. A great many students of world politics, including Ambassador Kennan, have doubted that this was ever the Russian purpose, even before the build-up of armaments by the West in the late forties and early fifties. What would the Soviet Union have to gain by the attempt to "conquer" the highly industrialized West? It would meet widespread hostility by both intellectual and working classes and could gain far more, both economically and politically, by refraining from military occupation. Already there is evidence that Russia has its hands full in Eastern Europe. Any "conquest" of the West would simply complicate its problems and endanger all its economic plans.

Russian Communism, moreover, is in a bureaucratic stage of development; its militancy is not what it was a generation ago. And it might be appropriate to note, too, that the tensions between the Soviet Union and China are such that it would be extremely hazardous for Moscow to take on new burdens in the West while allowing its eastern flank to be menaced by Peiping.

The prediction that the Soviet would in fact eventually respond favorably to the American initiative is based in some measure on the assumption that Soviet armaments are in part, as we have suggested earlier, an expression of Russian fears of the United States. As Herman Kahn put it: "The big thing that the Soviet Union and the United States have to fear from each other is fear itself."[3] If this is true, then Erich Fromm is right when he suggests that unilateralism "would most likely do away with this major cause" of war.[4] American psychologists like Ralph White would appear to agree about the crucial role of fear; and if they are right, the elimination of what the Soviet sees as the American military threat would tend to abate the fears which are expressed by Soviet armaments. This does not necessarily mean that the Soviet Union would immediately give up its arms but that it would at least cease to increase them and might, indeed, reduce them drastically. Nor does it mean that Communists would not continue to try to "infiltrate." But again it should be emphasized that military power is not the way to meet Communist economic and political aggression.

One of the greatest question marks is, of course, the People's Republic of China. Unilateralism, as we have said, would imply immediate negotiations for recognition of that Republic and an attempt to grapple with the problem of Formosa. This settlement might imply a plebiscite or an evacuation of those objecting to rule by Peiping. In any event, it is not primarily the military power of the West which keeps the People's Republic from expanding today. In general, where there is a danger of Communist take-overs in Asia, the result is brought about because of the collapse of old social and economic orders and an inability to discover new ones; Communism steps into this vacuum. The military power of SEATO, such as it is, will not

[3] Herman Kahn, *SRI Journal*, III (1959), p. 140.
[4] *Op. cit.*, p. 192.

be a primary factor in preventing Communist rule of Laos, for example, any more than it constituted a bar to Communist expansion into Tibet.

American unilateralism probably would not, to be sure, immediately induce the Chinese to reduce their armaments, any more than it would in itself help resolve the many political differences which exist between Peiping and the West. But again, the internal problems of China are so overwhelming that there would be little likelihood of American unilateralism leading it to "take over" nations remote from its territory or having little if any connection with it ethnically. And since unilateralism would imply a radically different spirit in American foreign policy, the possibilities of conciliation would seem to be much more promising under its aegis than within the context of present policy. In the long run, American military power cannot tame the aggressiveness of the Chinese regime: here, as elsewhere, it is useless. Only political, social, and economic measures which recognize the phenomenon of "rising expectations" can hope to check the appeal of Chinese Communism. So long as we continue to rely on military power, we are doomed to frustration.

In assessing the effects of unilateralism on the Soviet Union and China, we must above all remember that it would constitute a traumatic shock for the ideologies of both regimes. Marxism-Leninism predicts that "capitalist" systems will reply violently to the challenge of Communist power; and Communism is theoretically prepared to deal with this violent opposition. But a capitalist system responding after the manner suggested by unilateralism would find Communism with its guard down. Communist theoreticians would have to devise a whole new scheme of evaluation and would, no doubt, be greatly divided at first on what their response should be. The political split between the Soviet Union and China could be greatly enhanced; for there might be a tendency for Soviet Communist theory to differ quite sharply from Chinese doctrine in its judgments about American actions. Ideological considerations, it is true, are only partially responsible for the actions of so-called Great Powers; but they surely cannot be ignored.

Any realistic political analysis of the Soviet Union and of China will stress the diversity contained within their ruling elites. Remove what the Communists conceive to be the American military threat and these diversities and potential fissions, far from being eliminated, are likely to be exacerbated; for the threat of external military opposition has often tended to restrain the incipient factionalism of those states against which it is ostensibly directed.

Principled unilateralism, such as that suggested here, is far more likely to encourage relatively "open" societies than a policy based on military threats. The overt and obvious removal of the American military posture could do more to change the character of the Soviet and Chinese regimes than any other external measure. Basically, of course, fundamental undermining of autocracies is a matter for internal action and most certainly cannot be accomplished in the long run by external military threats. But if any external action could be efficacious, it would be a policy of unilateralism. This would be true if only because unilateralism would tend to strengthen the views of the "peaceful co-existence" advocates within the Soviet Union and China and to weaken the position of those who take a "hard" line.

As for the reaction of the non-Communist world, American unilateralism would doubtless provoke a very mixed reaction at first. The fact that it had triumphed in American politics, of course, might betoken that it had also made considerable progress elsewhere; for tendencies in one part of the modern world cannot be rigidly isolated from other portions. No doubt British opinion would be most receptive, if only because a unilateralist position of some kind had been espoused by considerable numbers in Britain for a fairly long period. Whatever the attitude of the British Cabinet initially, it would hardly expect realistically to put any reliance in its own weapons once the Americans had disarmed. To continue its armaments would be completely useless. No doubt British and American authorities would begin to collaborate in the development of nonviolent methods of defense.

In France and Germany, there would be rather violent opposition at first, despite the fact that the election campaign in the United States might have given a forewarning. As in the case of Britain, however, American disarmament would dramatically pose the question as to whether there was any point in preserving

French and German armaments. France, perhaps, might retain its armaments for a time: in other words, the association of armaments with "glory" might die hard. And French psychological uncertainty about the national future might aid and abet this intransigence. Similar observations might be applied, in part, to the recently rearmed Federal Republic of Germany. Eventually, however, considerations of economy and utility—particularly if we assume some Russian and Eastern European disarmament —would probably lead both France and Germany to turn to nonviolent methods of defense. In this, of course, they would be encouraged by unilateralist America. In the absence of American armaments, it would be absurd to expect France and Germany to "defend" themselves militarily against the Soviet Union— even more absurd than it is today.

In the United States itself, it is possible that organized opposition might develop among certain minority groups. At certain points—perhaps by the middle of the Second Phase, after it had become obvious that the policy-makers meant what they said—there might even be danger of a military *coup d'état* led by generals concerned about loss of status or honestly disagreeing with the new policy. Such a threatened coup could be met effectively by nonviolent resistance on the part of the labor movement and other supporters of disarmament. Just as the threatened Kapp Putsch in Weimar Germany of the early twenties was defeated primarily through large-scale strikes, so would any attempted coup in the United States have to confront men and women who had now been partially trained in the techniques of nonviolent action.

We cannot be certain, of course, that Communist and non-Communist worlds would respond along the lines which have been suggested here. Indeed, any realistic unilateralist policy would in part be designed to anticipate a response which might include attempted military occupation. If this should in fact take place, the main function of nonviolent resistance would come into play. While by reason of its very nature not calculated to be a weapon of aggression, it could be a most effective one for defense. Obviously, we must remember that just as no great power has ever disarmed unilaterally, so no state in the modern world has ever worked out deliberately a scheme for nonviolent defense. Yet even where nonviolent resistance has been used haphazardly, sporadically, and largely without preparation—as in Norway against the Nazis and in some measure against the Russians in Eastern Europe in 1953—it has shown amazing potentialities. Unilateralism in its systematic proposals for nonviolent resistance could magnify those potentialities almost without limit. To be sure, there is no assurance that it would succeed in every respect; but then the advocates of reliance on military power, on the basis of much experience with it, probably have far less assurance to offer.

No method of conflict, whether violent or nonviolent, is without its difficulties and ambiguities. But nonviolent resistance would almost certainly be less costly—both materially and psychologically—than violence; and it could hardly be less successful. (After all, half those who wage armed conflict always "lose," even in a technical military sense.) Even if one assume a long military occupation, for which the realist must indubitably plan, most human beings would still remain alive in preparation for the day when their children could be more effective in their nonviolent opposition; whereas a continuation of the arms race almost certainly means a Third World War with its wholesale destruction of humanity and its creation of conditions in which some form of dictatorship would become virtually inevitable. Tyrannies, moreover, do not last forever. Even if not opposed through nonviolent resistance, they tend to disintegrate from within. Modern war, by contrast, could bring virtually irreparable ruin. Thus unilateralism at its worst would seem to be better than a continuation of reliance on military power.

4

There are certain standard objections to unilateral disarmament with which we might deal briefly in conclusion.

NO PANACEA

It is sometimes said that unilateralists claim to have a panacea for the world's political ills. On the contrary, unilateralism is in no sense a panacea. At best, it would be an important and possibly an indispensable part of a whole complex of policies designed to minimize the risk of thermonuclear war and to provide a less tense atmosphere within which international problems could be solved. There are no magic keys for the solution of questions which beset the world.

THE PROBLEM OF POWER

Critics often maintain that "power" is ignored by the advocate of unilateral disarmament. But this is true only if one defines power relations very narrowly. Military power is only one species. A major element of the unilateralist argument is that since one variety of power has proven itself utterly useless and destructive, we must turn to others. The thory of nonviolent power, in all of its ramifications—international organization, redress of inequities, elimination of disparities in economic power, nonviolent resistance, and other elements—is designed to spell out the foundations of the alternatives. In one sense, it is the advocate of military power who is unrealistic; for he does not see that it can no longer be effective—if it ever was—and continues to react almost automatically to political crises in ways which imply that military power continues to be what it was in 1600.

THE RISKS INVOLVED

Some emphasize the enormous risks of a unilateralist policy. It is indeed true that the proposal promises no easy way out. The critic is right when he points out the possibility of military occupation and he is on solid ground when he suggests such hazards as concentration camps, suffering, and death. But these are also very real hazards in an arms race and its probable outcome. Did military preparation keep these terrors from France in 1940 or Poland in 1939 or the Soviet Union in 1941? And the Third World War would make the Second World War seem like fisticuffs by comparison. When military defense admittedly can no longer defend, it is high time that we consider alternatives, with all their risks.

THE NATURE OF THE OPPONENT

Unilateralists, it is often charged, fail to recognize the character of the opponent. He is hard, ruthless, and unbending and understands only the language of "force," it is said. Now there is much to be said for a realistic appraisal of the opposition, whether in national or in international politics. And it is true that the power structures of the Soviet Union and China embody many of the qualities attributed to them by the critic. But one can grant this fully and still question seriously whether military power, under modern circumstances, is the way to deal with such opposition. No ruling class, moreover, is ever monolithic, as we have suggested earlier. Granted this, the essential task of those who wish to undermine the power of a given ruling class is to discover the best method for encouraging its incipient divisions. The threat of military annihilation, experience seems to show, far from splitting a governing group, is more likely to solidify it. While unilateral disarmament provides no guarantee that the governing class will disintegrate, it does remove an important incentive for it to develop solidarity and popular support.

NEGOTIATION

Sometimes it is said that unilateralism reflects an unfounded despair about the possibilities of negotiation. In one sense this is true: it is utterly unrealistic to believe that we can resolve political tensions in any fundamental sense so long as we negotiate, so to speak, with hydrogen bombs under the table. So long, moreover, as we continue to believe that the military may be useful for defense we are unlikely to arrive at multilateral agreements on disarmament. In these senses, then, the unilateralist does despair of negotiation. But he also believes that if unilateral initiatives are pursued consistently and in the proper context, the break in the arms race would restore the possibilities of genuine negotiation. Tensions in the negotiating atmosphere would be vastly diminished while at the same time the existence of organized nonviolent power would provide more effective and less dangerous sanctions than under present conditions.

THE ROLE OF FORCE

Occasionally it is alleged that unilateralism implies the renunciation of all physical force and that it therefore stands on dubious "absolutist" foundations. Generally speaking, however, advocates of unilateralism are not absolutists in this sense nor is the position itself premised on the repudiation of all physical force. Physical force within carefully prescribed contexts may play a useful role; but it does not follow from this that military power is either useful or morally legitimate. The fact that both a child and the society may benefit from restricted use of physical force for corrective purposes does not legitimate the threat of annihilation or the waging of war.

ACCEPTABILITY

The critic may agree with the argument but contend that it is "unrealistic" to think that the American people or their rulers are likely to accept the policy. Now no one would contend that the present government of the United States is unilateralist. Nor is it likely to be within the next two or three years. But it is a fact that a good many have become convinced by considerations like those presented in this paper. If some are open to conviction, why not others? Moreover, the United States has a tradition of experimentation and a pragmatic outlook. It need not be tied to archaic policies forever. And its religious and moral tradition—indeed, the religious and moral tradition of the West as a whole—should lead it to question seriously any policies which rest on threats of mass annihilation.

It might be observed in conclusion that there have in fact been fundamental changes in outlook and practice during the past generation. Within a relatively short period, for example, our whole attitude to sex has been sharply modified. In 1932, Americans were opposed to Social Security; by 1939, it was almost universally accepted. As recently as two decades ago a peacetime conscription bill barely passed the House of Representatives; today, hardly anyone opposes peacetime conscription. And one could continue.

In view of all this, the unilateralist will ask, is it really so fantastic to believe that radical changes in military policy could conceivably occur within a few years, especially as the ghastly alternative comes to be fully understood?